Everything

You Forgot in

Accounting 1

A QUICK GUIDE

Howard J. Levine CPA

First Edition
© 2020 **Howard J. Levine**
ISBN: 978-1-7332595-3-8
Library of Congress Control Number: 2020911474

TABLE OF CONTENTS

INTRODUCTION

You study. You take a test. You pass the test. You are in another class or at work and now must apply what was on the test. You forget what you learned. Well, guess what? You are normal!

This book is designed for you, the normal person who took an accounting class and has a vague recollection of what you learned. You are presented with a question on a subsequent exam or are suddenly thrust into a job where you have to do some accounting, and you get that panic attack. We have all been there—thus, the purpose of this book.

In my accounting practice, as well as a professor, I consistently notice that people just don't remember basic accounting concepts. In many cases they had a great teacher, but it has been a while and they have forgotten a lot of what they learned. Looking up the concept on the internet, while initially a good idea and may answer the immediate question, does not help you remember the concept for next time. Going back to your college textbook may work, but those books are not written in plain English, and many times they confuse more than they help. Of course, asking a fellow student or coworker may do the trick, but you need more than just a quick answer—you need to review the basics.

The title of this book, *Everything You Forgot in Accounting 1: A Quick Guide*, tells it all. In these pages, you will find a description of many concepts you are familiar with but honestly don't recall. The book is written in simple English, with as little accounting jargon as possible; in other words, it will help you easily recall and retain the information. There are no questions or exercises, just information and examples to get you up to speed quickly.

Since this is a reference book, don't feel like you have to start with page 1 and read the book cover to cover. Glance at the table of contents or the index to discover what you are looking for and go straight there. Of course, you may want to review other areas, but don't feel like you have to read the entire book in order to get the most out of it.

Finally, and most importantly, this book is not a substitute for a financial accounting class, where you will learn these concepts and a lot more. In order to really learn accounting, you must practice, so don't think you can master the subject by just reading this or any other book.

If you want an easy-to-follow reference, you have found the right source.

ILLUSTRATIONS

BASIC PRINCIPLES

This chapter gives an overview of accounting assumptions and principles. These concepts are what is behind accounting standards and financial reporting.

The Role of the FASB and Others

If every business or organization could record and report financial data however it wanted, comparisons among companies would be difficult if not impossible. Thus, most businesses keep their books and prepare reports by following **generally accepted accounting principles (GAAP)**. When everybody follows the same rules, owners, investors and others can compare one organization to another.

The **Financial Accounting Standards Board (FASB)** has the primary responsibility of developing accounting principles in the United States. The FASB publishes *Statements of Financial Accounting Standards* as well as interpretations of these standards.

Because GAAP impact how and what companies report, standards are established according to a process that seeks and considers input from all affected parties, including owners, creditors and others. The activities and statements of the FASB are published and available online.[1]

International Financial Reporting Standards (IFRS) are a set of globally accepted financial reporting standards. Many countries permit, or require, IFRS for publicly traded companies.

The **Securities and Exchange Commission (SEC)** has regulatory and enforcement authority

---

[1] The pronouncements and more of the FASB are found at www.fasb.org.

for publicly held companies in the United States. While the SEC relies on the FASB and the accounting profession to establish accounting standards, in certain instances the SEC has also established specific rules. When there is a disagreement over major issues, the SEC may exercise its influence to resolve the dispute. The SEC also has enforcement powers, which helps maintain credibility in financial reporting.

Key Accounting Assumptions

There are six key assumptions that underly GAAP. The assumptions are:

1. economic entity;
2. going concern;
3. monetary unit;
4. time period;
5. objectivity; and
6. conservatism.

Economic Entity

The **economic entity** assumption says that the business or organization is separate from its owners. There are essentially four different types of entities:

1. A **proprietorship** is owned by one individual. Proprietorships comprise about 70% of business organizations in the United States, mostly small businesses. While the cost of starting a proprietorship is low, the amount available to begin is limited to the financial resources of the owner. In addition, owners of proprietorships have unlimited personal liability if something goes wrong and they are sued.

2. A **partnership** is similar to a proprietorship, except that a partnership is owned by two or more individuals or entities. About 10% of business organizations in the United States are partnerships. In addition to combining the skills and resources of more than one person, a partnership has some of the same advantages and disadvantages of a proprietorship.

3. A **corporation** is organized under state or federal statutes as a separate legal, taxable entity. Corporations account for about 90% of the total volume of business in the United States but are only about 20% of the number of organizations. Corporations are owned by stockholders and, as such, are able to obtain large amounts of resources by selling stock. A major advantage of a corporation is limited liability, which means that only the corporation, not the stockholders, can generally be held liable for corporate actions. For more about corporations, see Chapter 14.

4. A **limited liability company** (LLC) combines attributes of a partnership and a corporation. An LLC is a popular alternative to a partnership since it can have tax and liability advantages to the owners.

The choice of the type of entity is generally made when the business or organization is first set up. The type of entity can, however, be changed if circumstances warrant it.

Going Concern

The **going concern** assumption states that the business will continue in operation for the foreseeable future. This also means that the business will be around to fulfill contracts and commitments (see Example 1.1).

Example 1.1

A business that filed for bankruptcy or has a history of losses may not survive long. Also, the death of an owner or key executive could mean that the business may not be a going concern for long.

Based on this principle, if a business or other entity expects to close or be liquidated in the near future, GAAP might not be appropriate. In this case, the business uses **liquidation accounting**, which values the business at how much it will be worth if everything is sold and all of the debts are paid off.

Monetary Unit

The **monetary unit** assumption says that the results of a company's activities are reported in the currency of that country (the dollar in the United States). All changes in the purchasing power of the currency, such as inflation and deflation, are ignored.

Time Period

The **time period** assumption says that changes in an organization's financial position are reported over a series of distinct time periods, such as months, quarters or years. These artificial periods are called **interim periods**.

Any twelve-month period is a **fiscal year**. This can be a **calendar year** (January through December) or even a **52/53-week year** (generally used in retail businesses). Any twelve consecutive months, such as July 1 through June 30, would be called a fiscal year.

Objectivity

The **objectivity** assumption states that the accounting records and reports are based on objective evidence. No matter what bargaining goes on between a buyer and a seller, only the final agreed-upon amount is objective enough for accounting purposes. The reasoning for this rule is simple: if the amounts at which properties are recorded were constantly being revised up and down based on offers, appraisals, and opinions, accounting reports would be seen as unstable and subject to manipulation.

Conservatism

Conservatism is the policy of anticipating possible future losses but not future gains. This tends to understate rather than overstate how an organization is doing. The policy essentially says a company should "play it safe" (see Example 1.2).

Example 1.2

Businesses are given a choice of several options where the chance of occurrence is about the same. Based on the conservatism principle, they must record the option showing the smaller gain.

Key Accounting Principles

Under GAAP, there are volumes of principles. These are the five key accounting principles that provide the basis for many of the others:

1. Cost[2]
2. Revenue recognition
3. Matching[3]
4. Full disclosure
5. Materiality

---

[2] This is also called the *measurement* principle.

[3] This is also called the *expense recognition* principle.

There is one important distinction between these principles and the assumptions discussed earlier: each of these principles have an element of judgement in them, while the assumptions are pretty cut and dry.

Cost Principle

The **cost principle** says that an organization records something that they purchase at what they paid (their cost). Because this is an objective, verifiable amount, the cost is considered reliable and also conservative. Some, but not all, assets are subsequently valued at fair value (see Example 1.3).[4]

Example 1.3

Imagine a building is bought for $550,000; that is the cost that should be entered into the buyer's accounting records. It does not matter what the seller's asking price or the assessor's property tax valuation are or even if the buyer receives a higher offer the day after the building was purchased. The cost concept is the basis for entering the exchange price, or cost of the building, into the accounting records of $550,000.

If, after buying the building, the buyer accepts an offer and sells the building for $575,000, they then show the $25,000 profit. In keeping with the cost principle, the new owner would record what they paid, $575,000, as the cost of the building.

Revenue Recognition Principle

The **revenue recognition principle** says that an organization shows revenues (income) when the earning process is complete[5] and there is reasonable certainty that the amount will be collected, usually in cash. There are five steps in the revenue recognition process:

1. Identify the contract(s) with the customer.
2. Identify any contractual promises (called the *transaction price*) to deliver goods or services.
3. Determine the transaction price of the contract, including any variable consideration (such as a discount offered).
4. Allocate the transaction price to the performance obligations in Step 2.
5. Recognize the revenue when, or as, the organization satisfies each of the performance obligations (see Example 1.4).

---

[4] See Chapter 10 for a discussion of fair value.
[5] Technically, when the performance obligation (the promise to transfer goods or services) is satisfied.

Example 1.4

Say you purchase an iPhone for $900. To illustrate how Apple would recognize the $900 of revenue, here is how each of the five steps would work:

Step 1: The contract is for you to purchase a phone.

Step 2: Apple sells you not only the phone but also a warranty and customer service. They may also bundle the phone with a particular cell service. Each of these are separate contractual promises.

Step 3: The total price of the contract is $900.

Step 4: Each of the obligations (the phone, warranty, customer service and bundling) are valued, with the $900 price allocated to each of these items. Assume that the phone stand-alone selling price is $800, the one-year warranty is valued at $40 and the two-year customer service is valued at $60. Bundling might be valued at zero since you can change providers at any time.

Step 5: As the each of the obligations are satisfied, Apple recognizes the revenues:

- When you take possession of the phone, the $800 sales price is shown as income.
- The $40 you paid for the one-year warranty is shown as income over the twelve months that the warranty covers.[6]
- The $60 for the two years of customer service is shown as income over the following twenty-four months.

Matching Principle

The **matching principle** says that an organization matches its costs with its revenues. It is closely related to the revenue recognition principle (see Example 1.5).

---

[6] Chapter 5 discusses how these adjustments are made.

Example 1.5

If the $800 value of the iPhone in Example 1.4 cost Apple $600, that $600 cost is recorded when the phone is delivered.

The cost of the warranty and the customer service are allocated over the respective one-year and two-year periods. This matches the cost of these services with the period in which the revenues are recognized.

Under GAAP, accounting records are maintained on the **accrual basis** of accounting. This means that revenues are recognized when the earning process is complete, and expenses are shown when the cost is incurred (the organization owes it). The **cash basis**, which is sometimes used by small companies and for tax purposes, says that you recognize revenues when you receive the cash and you show the expenses when you pay the cash; in other words, the income and expenses follow the cash. A **modified cash basis** of accounting is essentially the cash basis with modifications for noncash charges, such as depreciation.

Full Disclosure Principle

The **full disclosure principle** says that an organization should provide enough information to influence decisions by external users (those outside the organization). Full disclosure includes:

- notes to the financial statements, which add insights about the organization's operations, accounting principles, contracts and any pending litigation;
- supplementary schedules and tables, which show more detail than on the financial statements; and
- comments on the face of the financial statements, which clarify the numbers or refer to other parts of the statements.

Materiality Principle

While not ordinarily thought of as an underlying concept, the **materiality principle** says that an organization records items that are significant, or *material*, to the understanding of the financial information. Something is material if, by including or correcting the information, this would affect the user's decisions. Materiality is a judgement call based on all of the facts and circumstances (see Example 1.6).

Example 1.6

Imagine you have a business with sales of $1,000,000.

- You discover that the sales are off $1. Would that affect a decision or how well the business is doing? Probably not.
- How about if the sales are off $100? Probably not.
- If the sales are off $1,000? Probably not.
- If the sales are off $10,000? Perhaps, based on other factors, such as if the business has a small profit or loss.
- If the sales are off $100,000? Most certainly yes.

CHAPTER 1 SUMMARY

- GAAP are the framework of accounting rules used in the preparation of financial statements.
- Due to its objective nature, historical cost is generally used when reporting the value of assets under GAAP.
- While there are many types of entities, in all cases an organization is assumed to be separate from its owners.
- Revenue is recognized when the earning process is complete.
- Expenses are reported in the same period as the revenues they helped generate.
- A transaction is immaterial if a mistake in recording the transaction would not result in a significant misunderstanding of the financial results.

BALANCE SHEET

Financial statements and the accompanying disclosures are the primary means of conveying financial information to investors and creditors, in addition to other internal and external users. The financial statements most frequently provided are the:

- balance sheet;
- income statement;
- statement of stockholders' equity; and
- statement of cash flows.

This chapter discusses the **balance sheet**,[7] which shows the financial position of the organization at *a specific date*. It is a snapshot of the organization at that period of time. The balance sheet has three parts:

1. **Assets:** What the organization owns.[8] Put another way, assets are the economic resources of an organization.
2. **Liabilities:** What the organization owes.[9] In other words, liabilities are obligations to another.

---

[7] Sometimes called the statement of financial position.

[8] Statement of Financial Accounting Concepts 6 defines assets as "probable future economic benefits obtained or controlled by a particular entity as a result of past transactions."

[9] Statement of Financial Accounting Concepts 6 defines liabilities as "probable future sacrifices of economic benefits arising from present obligations of a particular entity to transfer assets or provide services to other entities in the future as a result of past transactions or events."

3. **Owners' equity**[10]: What remains for the owners when all of the assets are sold and the liabilities are paid off.[11] In a corporation, equity is generally called **stockholders' equity**.

Basic Accounting Equation

Every balance sheet follows the following equation:

$$Assets = Liabilities + Owners' Equity$$

This is also expressed as follows:

$$Assets - Liabilities = Owners' Equity; or$$
$$Assets - Owners' Equity = Liabilities$$

The balance sheet consists of three sections, as shown in the following example:

---

[10] Another term for owners' equity is net assets. This term is used on nonprofit financial statements.

[11] Statement of Financial Accounting Concepts 6 defines equity as "the residual interest in the assets of an entity that remains after deducting the liabilities."

Sample Corporation
Balance Sheet
July 31, 2020

Assets

Current Assets:

Cash	$ 50,000	
Accounts receivable	13,000	
Supplies	1,400	
Inventory	18,450	
Prepaid rent	10,000	
Total current assets		$ 92,850
Equipment	11,000	
Less: accumulated depreciation	(400)	10,600
Deposits		1,000
Total Assets		$104,450

Liabilities and Stockholders' Equity

Current Liabilities:

Current portion of notes payable	$ 5,000	
Accounts payable	10,000	
Salaries payable	5,500	
Deferred rent revenue	750	
Taxes payable	283	
Total current liabilities		$ 21,533
Notes Payable	$ 45,000	
Less current portion shown above	(5,000)	40,000
Stockholders' Equity:		
Common stock, 4,000 shares		
issued and outstanding	40,000	
Retained earnings	2,917	
Total stockholders' equity		42,917
Total Liabilities and Stockholders' Equity		$104,450

Account Classifications

Assets

Assets are generally classified into two categories: current assets and noncurrent assets. Assets are usually shown in decreasing order of liquidity (how easily the asset is converted to cash).

Current assets are cash and other assets that are expected to be converted to cash or used within the next year or the normal **operating cycle**[12] of the organization, whichever is longer. Some examples of current assets, as found in an organizations' **chart of accounts**,[13] are as follows:

- **Cash:** Cash on hand at the organization and money in the bank. This includes not only physical cash but also bank accounts, cashier's checks and money orders.
- **Cash equivalents:** Short-term investments that will mature no longer than three months from the date they are purchased. Examples of these are money market funds and U.S. Treasury bills.
- **Short-term investments:** Investments that the company has the ability and intent to sell within one year (or the operating cycle, if longer). See Chapter 10 for details.
- **Accounts receivable:** Amounts due to the company from the sale of goods or services. See Chapter 7 for details.
- **Inventory:** Goods held for resale to customers. See Chapter 8 for details.
- **Prepaid expenses:** Cash paid for something, including a service, prior to using it. Examples include prepaying a six-month insurance policy and purchasing supplies for later use.

Long-term investments are assets not used directly in the operation of an organization. Examples include stocks and bonds. See Chapter 8 for details.

Property, plant and equipment[14] are tangible, long-lived assets used in the operation of the organization. Examples include machinery, computers, land, buildings and vehicles. See Chapter 11 for details on these and depreciation.

Intangible assets are assets that lack physical substance. Examples include patents, copyrights, franchises and trademarks. See Chapter 11 for details.

Other assets are those not included in any of the other categories. These include rent deposits and the value of insurance policies.

---

[12] The period of time from when the organization acquires the materials or services and collects the cash from the sale.

[13] The listing of accounts in the ledger. See Chapter 3 for more details.

[14] Also known as "fixed assets."

Liabilities

Liabilities are classified into two categories: current liabilities (discussed in Chapter 12) and long-term liabilities (discussed in Chapter 13).

Current liabilities are debts expected to be paid within a year or the normal operating cycle, whichever is longer. Some common current liabilities include the following:

- **Accounts payable:** Amounts owed to suppliers of merchandise or services, usually with payment due in a short period of time (thirty to sixty days).
- **Current portion of long-term debt:** The portion of long-term notes (see the following section) that is due within the next year or operating cycle, whichever is longer.
- **Short-term notes payable:** A written promise to pay a loan in the next year.
- **Unearned revenues**[15]**:** Cash received from a customer before the goods are delivered or the service is performed. Examples include prepaying legal bills and gift cards.
- **Accrued liabilities:** An expense that has been incurred but the amount has not yet been paid. Examples include salaries, interest and taxes.

Long-term liabilities are obligations that will be paid in more than a year or the operating cycle, whichever is longer. Examples include most car loans, mortgages, bonds and pension obligations.

Equity

For a corporation,[16] equity generally has four components:

1. **Paid-in capital:** The amount that the owners (stockholders) have invested in the company.
2. **Retained earnings :** A company's accumulated lifetime profits that have not been paid out to the owners. They consist of the net income (or loss) of the company, less any dividends distributed to shareholders, since the organization began. As discussed in Chapter 14, **dividends** are the distribution of profits to the owners of a corporation. They are never an expense.
3. **Other comprehensive income:** Certain revenues, expenses, gains and losses that change stockholders' equity but are not included in net income.
4. **Treasury stock:** Stock that the corporation has issued and then purchased back but not yet retired or sold.

---

[15] Sometimes called deferred revenues.

[16] Equity transactions are discussed in Chapter 14.

In a proprietorship, equity has only one category, generally called *owners' equity* or *capital*. Equity in a partnership also has only one category, generally called *partners' capital*. Similarly, equity in an LLC only has one category, generally called *members' capital*.

CHAPTER 2 SUMMARY

- Assets consist of all of the property that an organization owns.
- Liabilities consist of all of the amounts owed to others.
- Equity is what is left for the owners after paying back all of the organization's debts.
- The accounting equation is Assets = Liabilities + Equity.
- The balance sheet shows the financial position of the organization at a specific date.

INCOME AND RETAINED EARNINGS STATEMENTS

This chapter discusses the income statement and the retained earnings statements.

Income Statement

Another financial statement is the **income statement**,[17] which shows the revenues, expenses, gains, losses and net income or loss over a *period of time*. An example of the income statement follows.[18]

---

[17] Other terms for an income statement are: statement of operations; statement of revenues and expenses; profit and loss statement; and P&L.

Sample Corporation
Income Statement
For the month ended July 31, 2020

Sales revenue		$ 48,500
Cost of goods sold		32,000
Gross profit		16,500
Operating expenses:		
Advertising	$ 200	
Depreciation	200	
Insurance	700	
Rent	2,000	
Payroll taxes	800	
Salaries	10,000	
Supplies	500	
Total operating expenses		14,400
Operating income		2,100
Other revenue (expenses):		
Rent revenue	500	
Interest expense	(400)	100
Net income before taxes		2,200
Provision for income taxes		(283)
Net income		$ 1,917

Elements of an Income Statement

The major elements of an income statement are as follows:

Operating income: Items directly related to the revenue-generating activities of the organization.

    Revenues: Sales and other income generated from normal business operations, usually by providing goods and services to customers. Examples include sales revenue and fees earned.

    Cost of goods sold: The direct cost of the goods that are used in generating revenues. This usually corresponds to inventory or merchandise and is discussed in Chapter 8.

Expenses: Other costs of generating revenues. Common expenses are salaries, rent and insurance. Expenses are sometimes summarized in categories such as operating, selling and administrative.

Non-operating items: Items related to incidental activities of an organization. These are not part of the normal operating activities but still affect how the organization is doing.

Other revenues: Examples include interest, royalties, rent, dividends and gains from the sales of investments.

Other expenses: Examples include interest paid, litigation losses, and losses from the sale of investments.

Income taxes[19]: The portion of state and federal taxes applicable to the current reporting period.

Net income (loss): The sum of all of the revenues, less the total of all of the expenses. If the revenues exceed the expenses, it is **net income**; if the expenses are more than the revenues, it is **net loss**.

Another form of income statement is the single-step format. This format has two broad classifications—(1) revenues and gains and (2) expenses and losses—as the following illustrates:

Sample Corporation Income Statement For the month ended July 31, 2020		
Revenues and gains:		
Sales revenue	$ 48,500	
Rent revenue	500	
Total revenues and gains		49,000
Expenses:		
Cost of goods sold	$ 32,000	
Operating	14,400	
Interest	400	
Total operating expenses		46,800
Net income before taxes		2,200
Provision for income taxes		(283)
Net income		$ 1,917

[19] Also called *provision for income taxes*.

Retained Earnings Statement

In a corporation, the **statement of retained earnings** reports the changes in the retained earnings over a *period of time*. Because the net income or loss is reported on this statement, this statement is prepared after the income statement has been completed.

An example of the statement of retained earnings in a corporation follows.

Sample Corporation Statement of Retained Earnings For the month ended July 31, 2020		
Retained earnings, beginning of the month		$ 1,500
Net income	$ 1,917	
Dividends	(500)	1,417
Retained earnings, end of the month		$ 2,917

In a proprietorship this statement is called the statement of owners' equity; in a partnership it is referred to as the statement of partner's equity; and in an LLC it is termed the statement of members' equity. In all cases, the format is essentially the same.

CHAPTER 3 SUMMARY

- The income statement shows an organization's financial performance over a period of time.
- Revenues less expenses equal net income.
- The statement of retained earnings shows the changes in the organization's retained earnings over a period of time.
- Dividends are a distribution of profits, not an expense.

STATEMENT OF CASH FLOWS

The **statement of cash flows** shows where an organizations' cash was generated and where it was spent over a *period of time*. While this is a required statement under GAAP, many privately held organizations only prepare a statement of cash flows when they are required to, such as during a financial audit.

There are two methods that can be used when preparing the statement of cash flows: the **indirect method** and the **direct method**.

1. The indirect method adjusts the net income from the income statement[20] for changes in cash during the period. This is accomplished by analyzing the changes in the balance sheet accounts.
2. The direct method analyzes the changes for selected accounts from both the income statement and the balance sheet.

A sample statement of cash flows, using the **indirect method**, follows:

---

[20] See Chapter 3 for a discussion of the income statement.

Sample Corporation
Statement of Cash Flows - Indirect Method
For the month ended July 31, 2020

Cash flows from operating activities:		
Net income	$ 1,917	
Adjustments to reconcile net income to		
net cash flow from operating activities:		
Depreciation	200	
Changes in current operating assets and liabilities:		
Increase in accounts receivable	(1,000)	
Decrease in supplies	200	
Increase in inventory	(300)	
Increase in prepaid rent	(100)	
Increase in accounts payable	2,600	
Decrease in salaries payable	(200)	
Increase in deferred rent	300	
Increase in taxes payable	100	
Net cash flow from operating activities		$ 3,717
Cash flows from investing activities:		
Cash paid for purchase of equipment		(2,000)
Cash flows from financing activities:		
Cash paid on notes payable	(1,000)	
Cash paid for dividends	(500)	
Net cash flow from financing activities		(1,500)
Change in cash		217
Cash at the beginning of the month		49,783
Cash at the end of the month		$50,000

No matter which method is used, the statements of cash flows has the same three sections: (1) operating activities, (2) investing activities, and (3) financing activities.

Indirect Method

The indirect method begins with net income and, by primarily using changes in many of the balance sheet accounts, shows the changes in cash during the period.

Operating Activities

Cash flows from **operating activities** are changes in cash (both receipts, or inflows and payments, or outflows) from items reported primarily on the balance sheet. Using the indirect method, this section begins with net income and works backwards by converting the accrual basis net income to the cash basis (see Example 4.1). There are two sections of operating activities:

1. **Noncash revenue and expenses:** Because this statement is about cash flows, to arrive at the change in cash, any *noncash* items are either added back to, or subtracted from, net income. Common noncash expense items that are *added* back are depreciation, amortization and losses on the sale of investments or equipment. Common noncash revenue items that are *deducted* from net income are the gain on the sale of investments and equipment.

2. **Changes in current assets and current liabilities:** Changes in these accounts directly impact the net income of an organization. They are shown on the statement of cash flows as follows:

Description	Shown on Statement of Cash Flows As
Increase in current asset	Decrease in cash from operating activities
Decrease in current asset	Increase in cash from operating activities
Increase in current liability	Increase in cash from operating activities
Decrease in current liability	Decrease in cash from operating activities

---

Example 4.1

An organization's accounts receivable increases by $100 for the period. Sales, which are shown on the income statement and are part of net income, increased; however, the cash has not yet been collected. Thus, in order to show the cash flow of the organization, the net income is decreased by the $100 still owed but not yet collected.

Investing Activities

Cash flows from **investing activities** include the buying and selling of investments and fixed assets. These can be either increases in cash, decreases in cash, or both (see Example 4.2).

Example 4.2

An organization purchases a machine for $5,000 and sells a bond investment for $3,000. The $5,000 that they paid for the machine is a decrease in cash, while the $3,000 that they received for the bond investment is an increase in cash. These are shown as two separate lines in the investing section on the statement of cash flows.

Financing Activities

Cash flows from **financing activities** are related to the external financing of the company. Cash inflows include borrowing money and investments by the owners. Cash outflows include repaying loans and payment of dividends to the stockholders (see Example 4.3).

Example 4.3

An organization borrows $20,000 from the bank and pays back $15,000 during the year. While the net effect is $5,000, there is an increase in cash of $20,000 and a decrease of $15,000. These are both shown in the financing activities section in the statement of cash flows.

Noncash Activities

Organizations may occasionally have transactions that do not involve cash; these are called **noncash activities**. Examples include:

- the purchase of fixed assets with no money down and just a loan;
- organization costs paid for by issuing stock; and
- conversion of bonds to stock.

These items do not involve cash, so they are disclosed in a note to the statement of cash flows. Cash paid for interest and taxes, and any restrictions on cash, must also be disclosed.

Direct Method

The **direct method** has the same three classifications (i.e., operating, investing and financing cash flows) as the indirect method. The only difference is that the operating section of the direct method is based on the income statement, rather than the balance sheet.

Using the direct method, cash *inflows* from operations include cash received from:

- customers (from the sale of goods or services); and
- interest and dividends received from investments.

Cash *outflows* from operations using the direct method include cash paid for:

- the purchase of inventory;
- operating expenses, such as salaries, wages and rent;
- interest on debt; and
- income taxes.

An example of the direct method follows.

Sample Corporation
Statement of Cash Flows - Direct Method
For the month ended July 31, 2020

Cash flows from operating activities:

Cash received from customers	$ 47,000	
Cash paid to suppliers	(42,700)	
Cash paid for income taxes	(583)	
Net cash flow from operating activities		$ 3,717

Cash flows from investing activities:

Cash paid for purchase of equipment		(2,000)

Cash flows from financing activities:

Cash paid on notes payable	(1,000)	
Cash paid for dividends	(500)	
Net cash flow from financing activities		(1,500)
Change in cash		217
Cash at the beginning of the month		49,783
Cash at the end of the month		$ 50,000

CHAPTER 4 SUMMARY

- The statement of cash flows shows the changes in cash over a period of time.
- Cash flows from operating activities include transactions that affect net income.
- Cash flows from investing activities include cash transactions involving investments in securities and fixed assets.
- Cash flows from financing activities include cash transactions between the owners and creditors.
- Noncash and some other items must be disclosed.

DEBITS, CREDITS AND ADJUSTMENTS

I n order to keep the books and create financial reports, accountants summarize transactions. This chapter describes how the process works.

General Ledger and Accounts

An **account** shows the effect of a business transaction. The various accounts of a business are organized in a **chart of accounts**. The organization uses the items in the chart of accounts to record transactions in its **general ledger**, which is the record of all financial transactions within the company.

An account in the general ledger has three components, as the following illustrates:

Account Name & Number	
Debit / Dr.	Credit / Cr.
Dr. Balance	Cr. Balance

1. Every account has a name and, in many accounting systems, an account number.
2. The left side of the account is called **Debit** (abbreviated Dr.).
3. The right side of the account is called **Credit** (abbreviated Cr.).

The balance of the account is found by adding all of the debits and subtracting all of the credits. The balance is recorded on whichever side has the higher net number (see Example 5.1).

Example 5.1

Below is a summarized account with a number of debits and credits. The debit balance of $300 is arrived at by adding all of the debits and deducting the sum of the credits. If the credit side were higher, the balance would be shown on the right, or credit, side.

Cash	
200	
300	100
400	500
300	

Rules of Debits and Credits

The rules of debits and credits are based on the account classification (see Chapter 1 for typical accounts). Note that the increase side of an account is also known as the **normal balance**. The rules, and the normal balances, are as follows:

- Assets: Increases are debits; decreases are credits. The normal balance is a debit.
- Liabilities: Increases are credits; decreases are debits. The normal balance is a credit.
- Equity: Increases are credits; decreases are debits. The normal balance is a credit.
- Dividends: Increases are debits; decreases are credits. The normal balance is a debit.
- Revenues: Increases are credits; decreases are debits. The normal balance is a credit.
- Expenses: Increases are debits; decreases are credits. The normal balance is a debit.

A chart summarizing these rules follows:

Rules of Debits & Credits

Normal Balance Debit		Normal Balance Credit	

Assets

Debit / Dr.	Credit / Cr.
⇧	⇩
Normal Balance	

Liabilities

Debit / Dr.	Credit / Cr.
⇩	⇧
	Normal Balance

Dividends

Debit / Dr.	Credit / Cr.
⇧	⇩
Normal Balance	

Equity

Debit / Dr.	Credit / Cr.
⇩	⇧
	Normal Balance

Expenses

Debit / Dr.	Credit / Cr.
⇧	⇩
Normal Balance	

Revenues

Debit / Dr.	Credit / Cr.
⇩	⇧
	Normal Balance

Double-Entry Accounting

Journals are used for the day-to-day recording of accounting events taking place within an organization. Since no transactions get into the accounting records without first being entered into a journal, journals are sometimes called the *book of original entry* (see Example 5.2).

Example 5.2

A journal will generally look like this:

Date	Account	Debit	Credit
(Date)	(Account name debited)	xxx	
	(Account name credited)		xxx
	(Description of the transaction)		

When looking at a journal, there are columns for debits and credits, plus room for an explanation. Using **double-entry bookkeeping**, there will be at least two entries (and frequently more) in the journal. After an entry is made, there is one fundamental rule that always applies:

Debits = Credits

After journal entries are *entered*, they are *posted* to the general ledger. Each account in the general ledger summarizes these transactions, using debits and credits, and the balance is computed. After each account balance is determined, the total of the debit balances in the general ledger are compared with the total of the credit balances in the ledger to verify that the fundamental rule, debits = credits, works. If they agree, then the ledger is *balanced*; if the two totals are not the same, the difference must be researched and corrected.

The general ledger is the primary source for the balance sheet (Chapter 2), income statement and statement of retained earnings (Chapter 3), and statement of cash flows (Chapter 4).

Adjustments

Whenever financial statements are prepared, **adjusting entries** are recorded. These entries record changes that span more than one time period. No matter what date they are prepared and recorded on the books, adjusting entries are always dated as of the last day of the accounting period being adjusted.

Adjusting entries will always affect at least one account on the balance sheet (also called *permanent* or *real* accounts) and at least one account on the income statement (also called *temporary* accounts). As with all accounting entries, debits must always equal credits.

There are five types of adjusting entries:

1. Prepaid expenses
2. Unearned revenues
3. Accrued revenues
4. Accrued expenses
5. Depreciation

Prepaid Expenses

Prepaid expenses are costs that are paid in advance. These costs are shown as a current asset and shown as an expense (adjusted) as they are used (see Example 5.3). Common examples of prepaid expenses include supplies and insurance.

Example 5.3

An organization[21] pays $2,400 on December 1st for a twelve-month insurance policy. At the end of December, they have used up one month, or 1/12, of the insurance. At the end of December, an adjustment must be made to reflect that $200 ($2,400 × 1/12) has been used. The adjusting entry is as follows:

Date	Account	Debit	Credit
Dec 31	Insurance Expense	200	
	Prepaid Insurance		200
	Insurance expired ($2,400 × 1/12)		

Insurance expense is an account shown on the income statement, and prepaid insurance is an asset reflected on the balance sheet. At the end of December, the balance in the Prepaid Insurance account will be $2,200 ($2,400 less $200 used in December). This represents eleven months of insurance not yet used.

---

[21] In this and the following examples, note that debits equal credits and there is an explanation, showing the computation.

Unearned Revenues

Unearned revenues[22] are created when an organization receives cash from a customer before providing the goods or services. The amount received is shown as a current liability and shown as revenue (adjusted) as it is earned. Common examples of unearned revenues are contracts, magazine subscriptions and gift cards (see Example 5.4).

Example 5.4

On February 1st, you receive a $40 gift card to Del Taco, and you use $10 of it on February 25th. At the end of February, Del Taco makes an adjustment to show the revenues earned. The adjusting entry is as follows:

Date	Account	Debit	Credit
Feb 28	Unearned Gift Card Revenue	10	
	Sales		10
	Gift card used during the month		

Sales is an account shown on the income statement. The $30 balance of the gift card ($40 card less $10 used) is shown at the end of February as a liability on the Del Taco balance sheet.

Accrued Revenues

Recording revenues before they are billed to a customer are called **accrued revenues** (see Example 5.5). These can occur when a job is partially complete or the timing of an invoice does not coincide with the accounting period. Examples of accrued revenues include unbilled services, commissions and interest.

---

[22] Also called *deferred revenues*, this is discussed in Chapter 12.

Example 5.5

An organization has a contract to provide training services. These services will be billed on the fifteenth of each month at a rate of $50 per hour. As of June 30th, the organization had provided 25 hours of training, so they are owed $1,250 (25 hours × $50 per hour).

Although the June revenue of $1,250 will be billed and collected in July, the revenue was earned in June, so an adjusting entry must be made to show the income. The adjusting entry is as follows:

Date	Account	Debit	Credit
Jun 30	Accounts Receivable	1,250	
	Training Revenue		1,250
	Revenue earned (25 hours x $50/hour)		

Accounts Receivable is an account shown on the balance sheet, and Training Revenue is reflected on the income statement.

Accrued Expenses

Accrued expenses[23] are costs that an organization owes but has not yet paid (see Example 5.6). Since the organization typically does not get a bill, these liabilities are different from accounts payable, where a bill is received. Examples of accrued expenses include salaries, interest, rent and taxes.

---

[23] Also called *accrued liabilities*.

Example 5.6

An organization pays employees twice a month, on the 5th and the 25th. At the end of December, they owe employees $25,000, which will be paid on January 5th. Because they were earned in December, this amount is a December expense. The adjusting journal for the salaries owed follows:

Date	Account	Debit	Credit
Dec 31	Salary Expense	25,000	
	Salaries Payable		25,000
	December 31st salaries to be paid January 5th		

Salary Expense is an account shown on the income statement, and Salaries Payable is reflected on the balance sheet.

Depreciation

Depreciation is the allocation of the cost of an asset over its useful life.[24] While there are various methods for depreciating an asset, the adjusting entry is always the same:

Date	Account	Debit	Credit
	Depreciation Expense	xxx	
	Accumulated Depreciation		xxx
	Depreciation for the period		

Depreciation expense is an account shown on the income statement. Accumulated depreciation is a **contra-asset** (an asset with a credit balance) and is reflected on the balance sheet.

CHAPTER 5 SUMMARY

- A journal entry consists of both debits and credits.
- Debits always equal credits.
- Based on the type of account, there are specific rules for debits and credits.
- Adjusting entries are made to bring the books up to date.
- Adjusting entries recognize revenues and expenses in the period the goods are sold or the services performed.

CASH AND RELATED ITEMS

This chapter covers the basics of cash and related items, including:

- classifying cash and related items;
- petty cash; and
- bank reconciliations.

Classification

There are four classifications of cash and related accounts:

1. **Cash** is something that a bank will accept at face value. Examples include coins, currency, checks, deposits, the amount in a checking account, cashier's checks and money orders.
2. **Cash equivalents** are investments that will mature (come due) within three months of the date of purchase. They are usually short-term, highly liquid investments, such as money market funds and bills.
3. **Restricted cash** is cash that must be used for a particular purpose and is not available for general use. These restrictions may be legal, such as money set aside for collateral or held in an escrow account, or internally restricted, like funds set aside that will be used to purchase a building.

4. **Compensating balances** are legally restricted deposits at a lender's bank or financial institution, usually in conjunction with a loan. These amounts compensate the bank for granting the loan or extending credit.

Each of these items are generally shown separately as current assets on the balance sheet.

Petty Cash

Petty cash (sometimes called a petty cash fund) is an amount of money set aside to pay small expenses to avoid the hassle of writing a check. Petty Cash is also the title of the general ledger account, shown separately on the balance sheet, which shows the amount of the company's petty cash (see Example 6.1). The amount of petty cash will vary by company, and is usually between $50 to $1,000.

Example 6.1

- Paying the mail carrier for postage due on a letter.
- Reimbursing $13 to an employee for supplies purchased.
- Reimbursing $20 to a supervisor for buying the staff donuts .

These small payments add up. Instead of writing a check for each item, a petty cash fund is used. The expenses are recorded in the company's books when the petty cash fund is replenished.[25]

The first step in establishing a petty cash fund is to estimate how much cash will be needed in the near future for small payments. Once this is determined, a check for that amount is written and cashed. That cash is given to an employee, the petty cash **custodian**, who is authorized to disburse money from the fund. The custodian must periodically account for both the funds paid out and the cash still on hand (see Example 6.2).

---

[25] Since the funds are maintained at one amount, a petty cash fund is sometimes also called an *imprest* account.

Example 6.2

A custodian is given $100 for the petty cash fund on February 1st. The journal entry to record this is as follows:

Date	Account	Debit	Credit
Feb 1	Petty Cash	100	
	Cash		100
	Set up petty cash fund		

The custodian now has $100 cash to reimburse small purchases.

Petty cash is replenished either at set intervals or when it reaches a minimum amount. When a petty cash fund is replenished, the general ledger expense accounts that are debited are determined by adding up the petty cash receipts. A check is written, payable to petty cash, for the amount needed to bring the account back to the original amount (see Example 6.3). Any discrepancies are debited or credited to the account *Cash Short and Over*.

Example 6.3

An organization begins with a petty cash fund of $100. The custodian disburses $25 for office supplies, $20 for postage and $45 for gift reimbursements. At the end of February, the fund has a balance of $6.

Since the fund began with $100, and the custodian has receipts for $90, one would expect a balance of $10 in the fund ($100 – $25 – $20 – $45). The difference between the expected $10 and the $6 on hand means that $4 is not accounted for. This is shown as an expense on the income statement.

The journal entry to show the replenishment of the petty cash is as follows:

Date	Account	Debit	Credit
Feb 28	Office Supplies Expense	25	
	Postage Expense	20	
	Gift Expense	45	
	Cash Short and Over	4	
	Cash		94
	Replenish petty cash fund		

The $94 check is cashed, added to the $6 that the custodian has on hand, and the $100 balance begins again.

Bank Reconciliation

A **bank reconciliation** is an analysis of the differences between the balance a bank shows on their records and the balance of the cash account(s) in the general ledger.[26] A bank reconciliation should be done at least monthly. The reconciliation is divided into two sections:

1. The *bank* section begins with the balance according to the bank statement and ends with an adjusted bank balance.
2. The company (or *book*) section begins with the balance according to the organization's records and ends with an adjusted book balance.

When the amounts in the two sections agree, the bank statement is "reconciled."

---

[26] A bank reconciliation is done for every bank account in the general ledger.

Bank Section

The **bank section** of a bank reconciliation compares the bank statement with the books, focusing on what the bank is not reflecting, such as the following:

- **Deposits in transit:** Deposits listed on the books that the bank is not reflecting. Any deposits in transit are added to the amount according to the bank statement.
- **Outstanding checks:** Checks that have been written that the bank has not yet cashed. These are deducted from the amount according to the bank statement (see Example 6.4).

Example 6.4

Here is an example of the bank section of a bank reconciliation:

Sample Company
Bank Reconciliation
April 30, 2020

Balance from the bank statement		$43,359.25
Deposit of April 29, not received by bank		8,160.00
Outstanding checks:		
#1257	$10,625.00	
#1280	440.00	
#1298	876.93	
#1299	5,209.07	
Total outstanding checks		(17,151.00)
Adjusted bank balance		$34,368.25

Book Section

The **book section** of a bank reconciliation compares the bank statement with the amount in the general ledger (the books) (see Example 6.5). This section focuses on what the company, rather than the bank, has not recorded.

Additions include:

- collections of notes receivable or other items that have not yet been recorded on the books; and
- interest earned that is shown on the statement but not reflected on the books.

Deductions include:

- returned checks for non-sufficient funds (NSF) that the company did not record;
- bank service charges;
- check printing charges; and
- errors in recording items on the books.

Example 6.5

Here is an example of the book section of a bank reconciliation:

Sample Company
Bank Reconciliation
April 30, 2020

Balance from the general ledger		
Items on the bank statement not on the books:		$38,975.00
Additions:		
Collection of note receivable	$ 2,500.00	
Interest earned	17.47	
Total additions		2,517.47
Deductions:		
NSF check	6,159.22	
Bank service charge	150.00	
Check printing charges	275.00	
Error in recording check #1281	540.00	
Total deductions		(7,124.22)
Adjusted book balance		$34,368.25

Using Examples 6.4 and 6.5, since the bank balance and the book balance of $34,368.25 are equal, the bank statement has been *reconciled*. At this point, journal entries are made to bring the books up to date (see Example 6.6).

Example 6.6

Using Example 6.5, the entry on the books is as follows:

Date	Account	Debit	Credit
Apr 30	Sales	6,159.22	
	Bank Charges	150.00	
	Office Expenses	275.00	
	Accounts Payable	540.00	
	Note Receivable		2,500.00
	Interest Income		17.47
	Cash		4,606.75
	Bank activity for the month		

CHAPTER 6 SUMMARY

- A petty cash fund is set up to allow for small payments.
- The petty cash fund is reimbursed periodically.
- A bank reconciliation accounts for the difference between what the bank shows as the balance and what the books reflect.
- A bank reconciliation is prepared every month for each cash account in the general ledger.
- A journal entry is prepared to bring the books up to date.

RECEIVABLES AND UNCOLLECTIBLE ACCOUNTS

This chapter discusses:

- funds owed to an organization; and
- how to account for uncollectible accounts (also known as bad debts).

Accounts Receivable

Accounts receivable (sometimes called **trade receivables**) are the result of the sale of goods or services for amounts other than cash[27] in the normal course of business (see Example 7.1). Under the accrual method of accounting, accounts receivable are recognized when the sale is made, *not* when the cash is collected. Since they are generally collected within a year, accounts receivable are generally classified as current assets on the balance sheet.[28]

---

[27] The term frequently used is that the sale is "on account."
[28] This chapter covers the sale of merchandise; Chapter 8 discusses the cost of merchandise sold.

Example 7.1

A company makes a sale on March 1st for $1,000, with the term n/30 (the total amount, net, is due in 30 days). The journal entry to record this is as follows:

Date	Account	Debit	Credit
Mar 1	Accounts Receivable	1,000	
	Sales		1,000
	Sales on account		

The company makes another sale on April 1st for $1,000, but the term of this sale is 2/10, n/30 (2% discount if the invoice is paid in 10 days; otherwise, the net amount is due in 30 days). Because they expect the customer to take the discount, under the **net method**, the journal entry to record the sale and the subsequent cash collection are as follows:

Date	Account	Debit	Credit
Apr 1	Accounts Receivable	980	
	Sales		980
	Sale on account [($1,000 – 2% ($20) discount]		
Apr 10	Cash	980	
	Accounts Receivable		980
	Cash collected from April 1 sale		

If the company has a small or insignificant number of discounts, they can report the sale under the **gross method**. Using that method, the journal entries to record the sale and cash collection are as follows:

Date	Account	Debit	Credit
Apr 1	Accounts Receivable	1,000	
	Sales		1,000
	Sale on account		
Apr 10	Cash	980	
	Sales Discounts	20	
	Accounts Receivable		1,000
	Cash collected from April 1 sale less 2% discount		

Customers are sometimes given the right to return a product. **Sales returns** is the term used when merchandise is taken back; **sales allowances** are price reductions to keep a customer happy. These are frequently combined into one account: **Sales Returns and Allowances**.

Since the seller is not sure how much will be returned, the sale price recorded on the books is reduced for the estimated amount of the potential sales returns and allowances.[29]

Based on prior experience, the seller estimates the amount of expected returns and allowances and makes an adjusting entry, usually at the end of the accounting period. The entry will debit the income statement account **Sales Returns** and credit the balance sheet account **Refund Liability**. As the returns come in, the liability account will be reduced (see Example 7.2).

Example 7.2

A calendar-year business has sales on account of $100,000. The journal entry to record the sales is as follows:

Date	Account	Debit	Credit
Dec 31	Accounts Receivable	100,000	
	Sales		100,000
	Sales on account during the year		

Based on prior experience, they anticipate 2% of the sales will be returned. The journal entry to record the potential returns is as follows:

Date	Account	Debit	Credit
Dec 31	Sales Returns & Allowances	2,000	
	Refund Liability		2,000
	Estimated liability on returns ($100,000 x 2%)		

---

[29] This is based on the revenue recognition principle discussed in Chapter 1.

In January of the following year, $500 of merchandise is returned and a refund is given. The entry to record the refund is as follows:

Date	Account	Debit	Credit
Jan 31	Refund Liability	500	
	Cash		500
	Refund made to a customer		

The Refund Liability account will have a balance of $1,500 ($2,000 – $500) at the end of January.

Uncollectible Accounts

Not everybody can, or will, pay their bills, so credit losses are inevitable. These losses are called **uncollectible accounts** or, alternatively, **bad debts**.

Direct Write-Off Method

If bad debts are not expected to be significant, a company may recognize the uncollectible accounts when they determine that the amount is not expected to be collected (see Example 7.3).

Example 7.3

A customer was billed $10,000 for services in December. The customer did not pay, and their business disappeared the following March. The customer cannot be located. The journal entry to record this bad debt is as follows:

Date	Account	Debit	Credit
Mar 31	Bad Debt Expense	10,000	
	Accounts Receivable		10,000
	Write off bad debt		

While this method is not allowed under GAAP, the direct method is generally required for income tax purposes.

Allowance Method

In order to reflect how much of the accounts receivable the company expects to collect, a contra-asset account is used on the balance sheet. This account, called **Allowance for Uncollectible Accounts**, is an asset account with a credit balance. The difference between the accounts receivable balance and the allowance for uncollectible accounts is the **net realizable value** or the amount expected to be collected of the receivables. The formula is as follows:

Accounts Receivable – Allowance for Uncollectible Accounts =
Net Realizable Value

Balance Sheet Approach

One way to estimate the net realizable value is to use the **balance sheet approach** (see Example 7.4). This method looks at the amount that will ultimately be collected from the customer.

The balance in the allowance account is compared with the amount that is actually expected to go bad, and an entry is made to adjust the allowance balance. When the amount owed actually becomes uncollectible, that account receivable is reduced; if they surprisingly pay, this entry is reversed.

Example 7.4

A company has $500,000 of accounts receivable and the allowance for uncollectible accounts has a credit balance of $25,000. After analyzing their receivables, they determine that $45,000 of the receivables will not be collected. The entry to record this is as follows:

Date	Account	Debit	Credit
Dec 31	Bad Debt Expense	20,000	
	Allowance for Uncollectible Accounts		20,000
	Estimate bad debts ($45,000 – $25,000)		

At this point, the net realizable value of Accounts Receivable is $455,000 ($500,000 – $45,000 balance in the allowance account).

A customer, who owes $5,000, goes bankrupt in January. The entry to record this is as follows:

Date	Account	Debit	Credit
Jan 31	Allowance for Uncollectible Accounts	5,000	
	Accounts Receivable		5,000
	Write off balance owed		

This does not change the net realizable value of the accounts receivable but, rather, reflects the reduced amount that the customer will ultimately pay.

If the customer unexpectedly pays $1,000 out of bankruptcy in June, the entry to record this is as follows:

Date	Account	Debit	Credit
Jun 30	Cash	1,000	
	Allowance for Uncollectible Accounts		1,000
	Cash received from prior bad debt		

Income Statement Approach

An alternative but just as acceptable way to estimate bad debts is based on credit sales. The **income statement approach** uses the history of credit sales to estimate how much will not be collected (see Example 7.5). Based on this history, the company will use a percentage of the sales on account to come up with the estimate of the current year's bad debts.

Example 7.5

A company has $1,000,000 of credit sales and the allowance for uncollectible accounts has a credit balance of $25,000. Based on their past collection history, they estimate that 2% of these sales on account will not be collected. On December 31, the entry to record this is as follows:

Date	Account	Debit	Credit
Dec 31	Bad Debt Expense	20,000	
	Allowance for Uncollectible Accounts		20,000
	Estimate bad debts ($1,000,000 × 2%)		

At this point, the net realizable value of Accounts Receivable is $955,000 ($1,000,000 – $45,000 balance in the allowance account).

Some companies use a combination of these approaches.

Notes Receivable

A **note receivable** is a written promise to pay a fixed amount, on a fixed day, usually with interest (see Example 7.6). A note can be from a loan to another entity, from the sale of equipment, or extended payment terms from an account receivable.

Interest owed on a note receivable is computed as follows:

$$Interest = Amount\ owed\ (principal) \times annual\ rate \times fraction\ of\ the\ year\ (time)$$

Example 7.6

On July 1st, a company issues a $50,000 note receivable, with a 6% interest rate, due in 5 years. Interest-only payments are due every three months until the end of 5 years, when the principal balance must be repaid. The entry to record the note is as follows:

Date	Account	Debit	Credit
Jul 1	Note Receivable	50,000	
	Cash		50,000
	Issue note receivable due in 5 years		

The entry to record the first, and each subsequent, payment of interest is as follows:

Date	Account	Debit	Credit
Sep 30	Cash	750	
	Interest Income		750
	Interest earned ($50,000 × 6% × 3/12)		

When the note is paid off, the entry is as follows:

Date	Account	Debit	Credit
June 30	Cash	50,000	
	Note Receivable		50,000
	Repayment of note receivable		

In Example 7.6, since the note is due in five years, it is classified on the balance sheet as a long-term receivable. If, instead, it was for one year or less, the amount would be shown as a current asset.

As with accounts receivable, if a note receivable will not be collected, an allowance must be set up for the potential bad debt.

CHAPTER 7 SUMMARY

- Accounts receivable are recognized when the sale is made, not when the cash is collected.
- When accounting for discounts, the gross method, where the sale is net of any expected discount, is generally used.
- The balance sheet approach estimates bad debts based on how much each customer owes and adjusts the allowance account.
- The income statement approach estimates bad debts based on credit sales and records that amount as the bad debt for the period.
- Notes receivable, unlike accounts receivable, usually include interest.

INVENTORY: RECORDING

This chapter discusses:

- recording and measuring inventory;
- different inventory systems; and
- what costs are included in inventory.

Measuring Inventory

Inventory are assets that are held for resale, including those that are used in production and will eventually be sold. Inventory is generally sold within a year and is classified as a current asset on the balance sheet.

In a merchandising (such as retail) business, these goods are purchased and sold "as is," essentially moving the inventory from a manufacturer to the end-user (see Example 8.1). Unlike merchandising entities, manufacturing companies make the goods that they then sell.

Inventories of manufacturers have three components:

1. **Raw materials:** The cost of materials that will become part of the finished product.
2. **Work in process:** Products that have been started but are not complete.
3. **Finished goods:** Inventory that is completed and not yet sold.

Example 8.1

A bakery makes chocolate chip cookies. The bakery has each of these types of inventory:

Raw materials: Flour, sugar, butter, eggs and chocolate chips

Work in process: Mixing up the batter and placing it in the oven

Finished goods: Cookies ready to sell

The **cost of goods sold** are the cost of the inventory that has been sold to customers. Because inventory is a critical component of a company's operations, this number is separately shown on the income statement. The company's sales less the cost of goods sold is called the **gross profit**. This important number reflects the profit a company makes from selling its products before all of its operating expenses. The formula is as follows:

Gross Profit = Sales – Cost of Goods Sold

Units Included in Inventory

The measurement of inventory and cost of goods sold begins with knowing how many units of inventory the company has on hand. There are times, however, when determining if the company owns merchandise is not quite that simple.

Goods in Transit

A company may have purchased inventory and have a legal title but not yet received the product. Who owns these **goods in transit** is usually determined by industry custom and based on the following:

- If goods are shipped f.o.b.[30] *destination*, the buyer owns the inventory when the goods are delivered. The seller is responsible for the shipping, so these goods are considered part of the seller's inventory until delivered to the buyer.
- If the goods are shipped f.o.b. *shipping point*, the buyer owns the inventory when the carrier takes possession of the goods.[31] Thus, they are reflected on the buyer's books even though they have not yet been received.

---

[30] Free on board.
[31] Shipping of these goods is usually paid by the buyer.

Goods on Consignment

When a business gives their merchandise to another company to sell but still owns the inventory until the product is sold, this is a **consignment**. When the sale is made, the seller (*consignee*) sends the sale price, less a commission, to the business (*consignor*).

Since they own the goods, the consignor includes the unsold inventory on their books. The consignee does not own the inventory, so they never include the cost of the inventory on their records.

Estimated Sales Returns

Sales agreements frequently allow a return of inventory to the seller (see Example 8.2). In this case, the seller records a liability for the estimated amount to be refunded.[32] They also show the estimated cost of the inventory expected to be returned.

Example 8.2

A calendar-year business has sales on account of $100,000, with the cost of the merchandise sold totaling $60,000. Based on prior experience, they anticipate 2% of the sales will be returned. The journal entry to record the merchandise return is as follows:

Date	Account	Debit	Credit
Dec 31	Inventory – Estimated Returns	1,200	
	Cost of Goods Sold		1,200
	Estimated returns inventory ($60,000 × 2%)		

In January of the following year, $300 of merchandise is returned. The journal entry is as follows:

Date	Account	Debit	Credit
Jan 31	Inventory	300	
	Inventory – Estimated Returns		300
	Inventory returned by customers		

The Inventory – Estimated Returns account will have a balance of $900 ($1,200 – $300) at the end of January.

---

[32] Chapter 7 discusses the sales and receivable side of this transaction.

Amounts Affecting Inventory

The cost of inventory includes all necessary expenditures to not only acquire the goods but also get the product available for sale to customers. These costs include the purchase price and might also include freight, insurance and preparation of the inventory to be sold. These costs are added to the price of the inventory and not shown as an expense until the merchandise is actually sold.

Freight-In

If the buyer pays the freight charges, this is added to the cost of the inventory and is referred to as **freight-in**. If the seller pays the charges, this is not a cost to the buyer but, rather, a selling expense of the seller.

Purchase Returns and Allowances

When a buyer returns the merchandise, they reduce the amount of the inventory on hand. These are called **purchase returns and allowances**. The entry on the books depends on the inventory system used.[33]

Purchase Discounts

A buyer may receive an incentive to pay early, called a **purchase discount**. As illustrated in Example 8.3, this is recorded at the time of the purchase.

---

[33] The next section discusses inventory systems used.

Example 8.3

A company makes a purchase on April 1st for $10,000, with terms 1/10, n/30 (1% discount if the invoice is paid in 10 days, otherwise the net amount is due in 30 days). Because they expect to take the discount, under the **net method**, the journal entry to record this is as follows:

Date	Account	Debit	Credit
Apr 1	Inventory (Purchases)[34]	9,900	
	Accounts Payable		9,900
	Purchase inventory ($10,000 – 1% discount)		

When the payment is made, the journal entry to record this is as follows:

Date	Account	Debit	Credit
Apr 10	Accounts Payable	9.900	
	Cash		9,900
	Pay for April 1 inventory purchase		

If the company has just a few small discounts, they can report this under the **gross method**. In this case, the journal entry to record this is as follows:

Date	Account	Debit	Credit
Apr 1	Inventory (Purchases)	10,000	
	Accounts Payable		10,000
	Purchase inventory on account		

When they actually take the discount, the entry using the gross method is as follows:

Date	Account	Debit	Credit
Apr 10	Accounts Payable	10,000	
	Inventory (Purchases)		100
	Cash		9,900
	Pay for April 1 inventory purchase, less discount		

---

[34] The account debited depends on the inventory system used.

Inventory Systems

There are two types of inventory systems used:

1. The *perpetual* inventory system continually adjusts the inventory and cost of goods sold for materials purchased and sold.
2. The *periodic* inventory system only determines inventory values and cost of goods sold at the end of a reporting period.

Both of these systems are allowed under GAAP and will, at the end of a period, produce identical results. No matter which of these systems are used, a physical count of inventory is required to adjust the books at the end of a period to the amount on hand.

Perpetual Inventory System

Using the **perpetual inventory system**, inventory is continually adjusted for each inventory transaction, such as a purchase, purchase return, or a sale (see Example 8.4). Because of this, the books will reflect the amount of inventory on hand at all times.

In this system, whenever a purchase is made, it is debited to the Inventory account on the balance sheet. When a sale is made, the cost of the item sold is credited to the Inventory account, while the cost of the merchandise is debited to Cost of Goods Sold (an expense account).[35]

---

[35] The income statement using the perpetual system is illustrated in Chapter 3.

Example 8.4

A company makes a $5,000 purchase on October 1, with terms n/30. The entry to record this purchase is as follows:

Date	Account	Debit	Credit
Oct 1	Inventory	5,000	
	Accounts Payable		5,000
	Purchase inventory on account		

They return $500 of defective merchandise on October 10.

Date	Account	Debit	Credit
Oct 10	Accounts Payable	500	
	Inventory		500
	Return defective merchandise for credit		

On October 15, they sell merchandise with a cost of $1,000 for $3,000.[36]

Date	Account	Debit	Credit
Oct 15	Cost of Goods Sold	1,000	
	Inventory		1,000
	Sale of inventory		

On October 15, the books will reflect an inventory balance of $3,500 ($5,000 purchase – $500 return – $1,000 sale). The income statement will show the $1,000 cost of goods sold.

Periodic Inventory System

The **periodic inventory system** does not maintain a continual record of the inventory. Instead, the quantity and cost are determined, based on a physical count, at the end of an accounting period. The balance of the inventory account and the cost of goods sold are adjusted at that time.

---

[36] As discussed in Chapter 7, there is also an entry debiting Accounts Receivable for the $3,000 selling price and crediting Sales for $3,000.

Unlike the perpetual system, which has cost of goods sold as one line on the income statement, the cost of goods sold section in the periodic system is shown as follows:

Beginning inventory (carried over from the last accounting period)

+ Net purchases (see the following text box)

= Goods available for sale (amount that could be sold)

– <u>Ending inventory</u> (from a physical count of the inventory)

= <u>Cost of Goods Sold</u>

When using this system, "net purchases" includes any purchase discounts, purchase returns and allowances, and freight-in, as follows:

Purchases (inventory bought during the period)

– Purchase returns and allowances (inventory sent back to the seller)

– Purchase discounts (discounts taken on purchases)

+ <u>Freight-In</u> (freight costs paid by the buyer)

= <u>Net Purchases</u>

When using the periodic inventory system, rather than debiting Inventory for every transaction, the previously discussed accounts are used instead. Thus, the income statement of a company using the periodic inventory system has a different look:

Sample Corporation
Income Statement
For the month ended July 31, 2020

Sales revenue		$ 48,500
Cost of Goods Sold:		
Beginning inventory	8,000	
Purchases	30,000	
Purchase discounts	(500)	
Purchase returns	(1,500)	
Transportation-in	3,000	
Net purchases	31,000	
Goods available for sale		39,000
Ending inventory		(7,000)
Cost of goods sold		32,000
Gross profit		16,500
Operating Expenses		14,400
Operating income		2,100
Other revenue (expenses):		
Rent revenue		500
Interest expense		(400)
Net income before taxes		2,200
Income taxes		(283)
Net Income		$ 1,917

CHAPTER 8 SUMMARY

- Inventory are goods held for resale to customers or used in the production of these goods.
- Since there may be goods in transit or on consignment, a company may not have physical possession of all of their inventory.
- The cost of inventory may not only be the purchase price but could also include discounts and transportation costs.
- The perpetual inventory system continually keeps track of inventory quantities.
- The periodic inventory system determines the inventory and cost of sales at the end of an accounting period.

INVENTORY: COSTING AND ESTIMATING

This chapter discusses:

- inventory costing methods using the periodic method; and
- estimating inventory amounts.

Inventory Cost Methods

Once a business knows the quantity of goods on hand, it must then determine the cost for each item. Under GAAP, there are four methods to determine the cost:

1. *Specific identification:* This method is used for unique, sometimes expensive products with low sales volume. This allows the cost of specific each unit sold to be traced. For example, each auto has a unique VIN (vehicle identification number), so the cost of each specific car is known.
2. *First In, First Out (FIFO):* This method assumes that the *first* units produced are the *first* ones sold. Beginning inventory is sold first, followed by, in the order that they are acquired, the next purchases during the period. For example, a grocery store would want to sell the oldest milk first, since otherwise it would spoil, thus using the FIFO method.
3. *Last In, First Out (LIFO):* This method assumes that the *last* units purchased are the *first* ones sold; in other words, the opposite of FIFO. In reality, virtually no company sells its merchandise this way, but they are allowed to use this method to value inventory.

4. *Average Cost:* This method assumes that the cost of the inventory and cost of goods sold are a mixture of everything purchased. An example is a bin of screws at a hardware store; each screw is identical and does not spoil, so there is no difference between the screws at the top of the bin and the ones at the bottom.

First In, First Out (FIFO)

The **First In, First Out (FIFO)** method treats the first goods purchased or manufactured (first in) as the first ones sold (first out). Thus, the ending inventory value reflects the most recent purchases.

To determine the amount of the ending inventory, you begin with the *most recent* purchases until you have accounted for the total inventory quantity. You then subtract the ending inventory cost from the total goods available for sale to arrive at the cost of goods sold. This is illustrated in Example 9.1.

Example 9.1

A company[37] has the following transactions in March:

Date	Description	Unit Price	Units Purchased	Units Sold	Units on Hand	Inventory Cost
Mar 1	Beginning inventory	$1.00[d]	200			$200
Mar 9	Purchase	$1.10[c]	300		500	330
Mar 10	Sale			400	100	
Mar 15	Purchase	$1.16[b]	400		500	464
Mar 18	Sale			300	200	
Mar 24	Purchase	$1.26[a]	100		300	126
	Total goods available for sale		1,000[f]			$1,120[c]

---

[37] This data will be used in examples throughout this chapter.

Using FIFO, to compute the cost of the units on hand, you start with the most recent purchase and work backwards until the total balance (300 in this case) is accounted for:

Date	Units	Cost per Unit	Total Cost
Mar 24	100	$1.26[a]	$126
Mar 15	200	$1.16[b]	232
Total cost			$358[d]

Cost of Goods Sold is computed by taking the goods available for sale less the ending inventory:

Goods available for sale	$1,120[c]
Less ending inventory	(358)[d]
Cost of goods sold	$762

Last In, First Out (LIFO)

The **Last In, First Out (LIFO)** method treats the last goods purchased or manufactured (last in) as the first ones sold (first out). Thus, the ending inventory reflects the oldest purchases.

To determine the amount of the ending inventory, you begin with the *oldest* purchases until you have accounted for the total inventory quantity. You then subtract the ending inventory cost from the total goods available for sale to arrive at the cost of goods sold. This is illustrated in Example 9.2.

Example 9.2

Using the data from Example 9.1 and using LIFO, to compute the cost of units on hand, you start with the oldest purchase and work forwards until the total balance (300 in this case) is accounted for:

Date	Units	Cost per Unit	Total Cost
Jan 1	200	$1.00[d]	$200
Jan 9	100	$1.10[c]	110
Total cost		$310[e]	

Cost of Goods Sold is computed by taking the goods available for sale less the ending inventory:

Goods available for sale	$1,120
Less ending inventory	(310)[e]
Cost of goods sold	$810

Average Cost

The **average cost** method uses an average cost to compute both the ending inventory and the cost of goods sold. Since all purchases and sales are combined, an average is taken and applied to both the ending inventory and the cost of goods sold (see Example 9.3). The formula to compute the average cost is as follows:

Average cost per unit = Cost of goods available for sale ÷
Units available for sale

Example 9.3

Using the data from Examples 9.1 and 9.2:

Cost of goods available for sale ($1,120)[c] ÷ Units available for sale (1,000)[f] = $1.12 average cost per unit.

Ending inventory is 300 units × $1.12 per unit = $336

Cost of Goods Sold is computed by taking the goods available for sale less the ending inventory:

Goods available for sale	$1,120
Less ending inventory	(336)
Cost of goods sold	$784

Inventory Write-Down

Occasionally, companies will sell inventory at prices below the cost. This might happen because the inventory is damaged or obsolete. When the value of the inventory is estimated to have fallen below its cost, they must adjust (write-down) the inventory amount to the lower amount.[38]

Lower of Cost or Net Realizable Value

Companies that use FIFO and average cost report inventory at the **lower of cost or net realizable value (NRV)**. NRV is the estimated selling price of the item less any costs of completion, disposal and selling, such as commissions and shipping costs. The company then compares the cost with the NRV, and if the NRV is lower, they adjust the inventory to the lower amount (see Example 9.4). This can be done either to individual inventory items, major categories or the inventory as a whole.

---

[38] As discussed in Chapter 1, this is based on the conservatism principle.

Example 9.4

A company has inventory that costs $910 and can be sold for $1,000. They estimate that the shipping costs will be about 10% of the selling price. Since the NRV is $900 ($1,000 – $100), and that is smaller than the cost, they must make an entry to reduce the inventory to the lower amount:

Date	Account	Debit	Credit
Dec 31	Cost of Goods Sold	100	
	Inventory		100
	Reflect write-down of inventory to NRV		

Lower of Cost or Market Value

Companies that use the LIFO method report at the **lower of cost or market value (LCM).** Market value is the replacement cost of the item, with some adjustments.

As with NRV, this amount is compared with the cost to individual inventory items, major categories or the inventory as a whole. The inventory is then adjusted to account for the write-down.

Estimating Inventory

It is occasionally problematic, or even impossible, to count inventory quantities at the end of a period. For example, if the inventory was destroyed by a fire or natural disaster, or a retail company has stores all over the nation and sells many different items, counting can be difficult.

Two methods of estimating inventory are the gross profit and the retail method. Since these are estimates. they are not acceptable costing techniques under GAAP. Either of these methods can, however, be used for interim financial statements and reporting insurance claims.

Gross Profit Method

If a company has a fairly stable gross profit, the **gross profit method** can be used either on the inventory as a whole or in a specific department. When a company uses the periodic system[39] and knows their usual gross profit, they can estimate the ending inventory, as in Example 9.5.

---

[39] The periodic system is discussed in Chapter 8.

Example 9.5

A company has its inventory destroyed by a natural disaster. They began the year with an inventory cost of $300,000. During the year they made purchases of $750,000 and had sales of $1,000,000 up until the disaster. Based on past years, the gross profit has been about 40%.

An estimate of the ending inventory is as follows:

Beginning inventory*		$ 300,000
+ Purchases		750,000
= Goods available for sale		1,050,000
Cost of Goods Sold:		
Sales*	$1,000,000	
– Estimated gross profit (40%)*	(400,000)	
= Estimated cost of goods sold (60%)		(600,000)
= Estimated ending inventory		$450,000

* From the general ledger

Retail Method

Companies that have high-volume sales with many different low-cost items may find that taking a physical inventory throughout the year is time-consuming and costly. These companies use the **retail method** to estimate their inventories.

This method begins with deducting the sales (on the books at the sale price) from the goods available for sale (on the books at both cost and retail, or selling, price). By doing this, the company estimates the ending inventory at the selling price. Since accounting records are based on the cost, not the retail value, this amount is multiplied by the ratio of the goods available for sale at cost to the goods available for sale at retail. The result of this is an estimate of the ending inventory, as illustrated in Example 9.6.

Example 9.6

A company has the following data:

	Cost	Retail
Goods available for sale:		
Beginning inventory*	$500	$900
+ Purchases*	6,500	9,100
= Total goods available for sale	$7,000	10,000
– Deduct net sales*		(8,500)
= Estimated inventory at the selling price		1,500
× Cost to retail percentage ($7,000 ÷ $10,000)		× 70%
= Estimated inventory at cost		$1,050

* From the general ledger

CHAPTER 9 SUMMARY

- There are four inventory costing methods: specific identification, FIFO, LIFO and average cost.
- Ending inventory and cost of goods sold will vary based on the method chosen.
- After computing the inventory at cost, this is compared to the lower of the cost or net realizable, or market, value, and an adjustment is made to reflect the lower amount.
- Inventory amounts can be estimated based on the gross profit or the retail methods.

INVESTMENTS

Companies invest for a variety of reasons, including earning income and for corporate strategy, such as mergers and acquisitions. This chapter discusses how an investing company accounts for two types of investments: debt and equity.

Debt Investments

A **debt investment** is essentially a loan that a company funds. The one who owes the money (the issuer) pays periodic interest to the investor. They also repay the loan to the investor at a specified date in the future, known as the **maturity date**. The issuing company shows the debt on their balance sheet as a liability; the investing company reflects the investment on their balance sheet as an asset.

Purchase

When debt investments are purchased, they are recorded by the investing company at the total amount paid, including any brokerage fees. When buying (or investing in) debt, the **contractual interest rate** (the interest rate the debt is paying) is compared with the current market interest rate[40]:

If the contract rate = market rate, the debt is issued at the **face value**.

If the contract rate > market rate, the debt will sell at a **premium**.

If the contract rate < market rate, the debt will sell at a **discount**.

---

[40] Note that these are the exact opposite of how an issuer prices bonds, as discussed in Chapter 13.

Bonds purchased at face value are priced, in bond language, at 100 (i.e., 100%). If a bond is purchased at a premium, the cost is shown as a number over 100 (i.e., 102, meaning 102% or 1.02). If a bond is purchased at a discount, the cost is shown as a number under 100 (i.e., 99, meaning 99% or .99) (see Example 10.1).

Example 10.1

On March 31, a company makes a $100,000 investment in a 5-year corporate bond. The market rate is 4% and the bond pays 3%; because the market rate is higher than the contractual rate, the bond is sold at a discount and priced at 98. The entry to record this investment is as follows:

Date	Account	Debit	Credit
Mar 31	Investments	100,000	
	Discount on Bond Investment		2,000
	Cash		98,000
	Purchase investment ($100,000 × .98)		

Interest

Since bonds are debt, they pay the investor periodic **interest**. The formula to compute interest is as follows:

$$Interest = Face\ value \times contract\ rate \times time\ period$$

If the bond is issued at anything other than face value, the premium or discount is written off (amortized) over the term of the bond (see Example 10.2).

Example 10.2

Using Example 10.1, when the semi-annual interest is paid on September 30, the entry is as follows:

Date	Account	Debit	Credit
Sep 30	Cash [a]	1,500	
	Discount on Bond Investment [b]	200	
	Interest Revenue [c]		1,700
	[a] Six months interest ($100,000 × 3% × 6/12)		
	[b] Discount amortization ($2,000 ÷ 10 periods)		
	[c] Interest revenue is the sum of these two		

Sale

Since this is an investment, if the bond is **sold** prior to the maturity date, a gain or loss is recognized on the books (see Example 10.3).

Example 10.3

On September 30, they sell the $100,000 investment in a corporate bond purchased (see Example 10.2). Interest rates have dropped, and they are able to sell the bond for 99. The entry to record the sale is as follows:

Date	Account	Debit	Credit
Sep 30	Cash [a]	99,000	
	Discount on Bond Investment [b]	1,800	
	Investments		100,000
	Gain on sale of investment [c]		800
	[a] Sale price ($100,000 × .99)		
	[b] Discount balance ($2,000 – $200)		
	[c] Difference is the gain on the sale		

Equity Investments

Companies will make **equity investments** in another company, usually their stock, for investment or strategic reasons. When making an equity investment, the accounting treatment depends on the degree of control that the investor has over the other company:

Percent of Ownership	Degree of Influence	Accounting Method
Less than 20%	No control	Cost
20% to 50%	Significant	Equity
More than 50%	Control	Consolidation[41]

Cost Method

Under the **cost method**, it is assumed that the company buys stock primarily to earn dividends or show a profit when the stock is sold. The accounting is similar to the purchase and sale of any other asset, as illustrated in Example 10.4.

---

[41] Consolidation accounting is not covered in this book.

Example 10.4

On May 1, a company buys 1,000 shares of stock at $30 per share. They own less than 20% of the company, so it is accounted for under the cost method. The entry to record this purchase is as follows:

Date	Account	Debit	Credit
May 1	Investments	30,000	
	Cash		30,000
	Purchase 1,000 shares at $30 per share		

On July 31, they receive a dividend of $1 per share.

Date	Account	Debit	Credit
Jul 31	Cash	3,000	
	Dividend Revenue		3,000
	Receive $1 per share dividend		

They sell the stock for $31 per share on January 15.

Date	Account	Debit	Credit
Jan 15	Cash	31,000	
	Investments		30,000
	Gain on Sale of Investments		1,000
	Show sale of stock at $31 per share		

Equity Method

Under the **equity method**, the initial investment is recorded at the cost. The investor's share of not only the dividends but also the net income is recorded on the balance sheet in the investment account, instead of on the income statement (see Example 10.5).

Example 10.5

On May 1, a company buys 1,000 shares of stock at $30 per share. This represents 30% of the company, so it is accounted for under the equity method. The entry to record this purchase is as follows:

Date	Account	Debit	Credit
May 1	Investments	30,000	
	Cash		30,000
	Purchase 1,000 shares at $30 per share		

On July 31, they receive a dividend of $1/share.

Date	Account	Debit	Credit
Jul 31	Cash	3,000	
	Investments		3,000
	Receive $3 per share dividend		

The company net income for the year is $50,000.

Date	Account	Debit	Credit
Dec 31	Investments	15,000	
	Investment Income		15,000
	Show share of profits ($50,000 × 30%)		

They sell the stock for $45/share on January 15.

Date	Account	Debit	Credit
Jan 15	Cash	45,000	
	Investments		42,000
	Gain on sale of stock		3,000
	Show sale of stock at $45 per share		

The investment account balance of $42,000 is computed as the cost ($30,000) less the dividend received ($3,000) plus the share of net income ($15,000). The gain is the difference between the cash received and the balance in the investment account.

Reporting Investments

Most debt and equity investments are publicly traded. Because of this, GAAP allows these investments to be reported at their fair market value.

Trading Securities

Trading securities are stocks and bonds usually held for a short period of time with the intent to sell; they are shown as current assets on the balance sheet. Trading securities are reported at **fair value**—that is, the market price a company would get if the investment was sold at the balance sheet date. Any increase or decrease from the cost is shown as an **unrealized gain or loss** on the income statement (see Example 10.6).

Example 10.6

A company has a portfolio of securities that they purchased for $50,000. On September 30, the value of these securities is $52,000. The entry to record this is:

Date	Account	Debit	Credit
Sep 30	Investments	2,000	
	Unrealized Gain on Investments		2,000
	Show unrealized gain ($52,000 – $50,000)		

Available for Sale Securities

Securities that are not trading securities are **available for sale**. Rather than on the income statement, changes in the fair value of these are generally shown as an increase in the "other comprehensive income" portion of the stockholder's equity section[42] on the balance sheet.

Held to Maturity Securities

Held to maturity securities are debt investments that a company intends to earn interest revenue and hold until the securities mature. If these investments will come due within a year, they are classified as current assets on the balance sheet; if they mature in more than a year, they are

---

[42] This section of a corporation's balance sheet is discussed in Chapter 14.

shown as noncurrent assets. These investments are reported at their amortized cost (the face value less any unamortized premium or plus any unamortized discount).

CHAPTER 10 SUMMARY

- Organizations make investments for a variety of reasons and record the cost of the investment when it is made.
- Debt instruments are loans made to another entity, earn interest and are repaid at a future date.
- Equity investments are investments in another company, and the method of accounting depends on the level of control the investor has.
- Based on how management intends on using the investments, the investments are reported on either the balance sheet or the income statement.

PROPERTY, PLANT, EQUIPMENT AND INTANGIBLE ASSETS

This chapter covers the following:

- Types of property, plant and equipment and their cost
- Depreciation and depletion
- Disposition of property plant and equipment
- Intangible assets and amortization

Categories of Fixed Assets

Property, plant and equipment, also called **fixed assets**, are assets that are used in the company's operations, have physical substance and should last a long time. In addition to the purchase price, the cost of these assets includes any additional expenditures to get the asset in condition so it can be used (see Example 11.1).

Fixed assets include:

- *Land.* Real property used in the business (as opposed to held for investment). Typical costs for acquiring land include the purchase price, escrow fees, clearing the land and removing old buildings.
- *Land improvements.* Enhancements to land, such as parking lots, driveways, private roads, sprinkler systems and fences.

- *Buildings.* Permanent or temporary structures used in the business. Costs include the purchase price, escrow fees and reconditioning. Note that the cost of a building is always shown separately from the land.
- *Equipment.* Property used in the operations of the business, such as machinery, computers, equipment, vehicles and furniture. Costs of equipment include the purchase price, sales tax, transportation, installation and testing.
- *Natural resources.* Assets that are physically used, such as timber, oil, gas and mineral deposits. Costs include acquisition, exploration, development and restoration expenditures.

Example 11.1

A company purchases a piece of equipment on July 1 costing $50,000. That cost, plus the sales tax ($4,500), shipping ($2,000) and testing ($1,500) are all added to the cost of the fixed asset. The journal entry to record this purchase is as follows:

Date	Account	Debit	Credit
Jul 1	Equipment	58,000	
	Cash		58,000
	Show equipment purchase		

The following items are *not* fixed assets:

- *Repairs.* Since ordinary repairs are an ongoing cost of business, they are shown as an expense in the period incurred. Major expenditures that extend the life of an asset, however, are capitalized.
- *Research and development.* Research and development costs are generally shown as an expense incurred.
- *Immaterial amounts.* If a cost is so small that it would not significantly impact the financial statements, these are not recorded as fixed assets but, rather, shown as an expense. Many companies have a **capitalization policy**, which is a dollar limit below the expensed fixed assets (see Example 11.2).

Example 11.2

A company with a capitalization policy of $2,500 spends $20 for a new stapler. Although a stapler will last many years and fits into the technical definition of a fixed asset, because the amount is so small, it would be silly to capitalize this asset. Thus, this purchase is shown as an expense on the income statement.

Depreciation

Depreciation is the process of allocating the cost of a fixed asset over its estimated useful life. The **estimated useful life** of an asset is the period the company plans to use the asset. Finally, the **residual** (or salvage) value is the estimated amount the company might get from disposal or trade-in of the asset at the end of its useful life.

The journal entry for depreciation is always exactly the same:
Depreciation expense xxx
    Accumulated depreciation xxx

Accumulated depreciation is a contra-asset account, which is an asset account with a *credit* balance. The cost of an asset less the accumulated depreciation is called the **book value** of the asset. Note that this is *not* the market value, just the value per the books. Nothing else.

Book Value = Cost – Accumulated Depreciation

There are three commonly used **methods** for depreciating a fixed asset: (1) straight-line method; (2) units-of-production method; and (3) declining-balance method.

Straight-Line Method

The straight-line method uses the same depreciation amount over the life of the asset (see Example 11.3). The computation is as follows:

*Annual depreciation = (Cost of the asset – salvage value) ÷
Estimated useful life*

Example 11.3

Equipment is purchased on January 1 for $11,000. It has a residual value of $1,000 and is expected to last 5 years. The journal entry to record the annual depreciation is as follows:

Date	Account	Debit	Credit
Dec 31	Depreciation Expense	2,000	
	Accumulated Depreciation		2,000
	Depreciation for the year ($10,000 ÷ 5 years)		

At this point, the book value would be $9,000 ($11,000 cost less $2,000 accumulated depreciation). At the end of 5 years, the book value will be the $1,000 residual value.

If the asset was purchased on July 1, the depreciation would be for half a year, or $1,000.

Units-of-Production Method

The units-of-production method matches the allocation of the cost of an asset with its volume or output during the year (see Example 11.4). The computation is as follows:

*Annual depreciation = (Cost of the asset – salvage value) ×
Units used during the year ÷ Estimated units
to be used over the useful life*

Example 11.4

A truck is purchased on July 1 for $110,000. It has a residual value of $10,000 and is expected to be driven for 200,000 miles. In the current year, the truck is driven 20,000 miles. The journal entry to record the first-year depreciation is as follows:

Date	Account	Debit	Credit
Dec 31	Depreciation Expense	10,000	
	Accumulated Depreciation		10,000
	Depreciation for the year		
	($100,000 × 20,000 miles) ÷ 200,000 miles		

At this point, the book value would be $100,000 ($110,000 cost less $10,000 accumulated depreciation).

Declining-Balance Method

The declining-balance method assumes that the usefulness of an asset declines as the asset gets older (see Example 11.5). The most common declining-balance method is double-declining-balance, which is computed as follows:

Annual depreciation = Beginning of the year book value ÷ (Estimated useful life × 2)

Example 11.5

Equipment is purchased on January 1 for $11,000. It has a residual value of $1,000 and is expected to last 5 years. The journal entry to record the first-year depreciation is as follows:

Date	Account	Debit	Credit
Dec 31	Depreciation Expense	4,400	
	Accumulated Depreciation		4,400
	Depreciation for the year		
	($11,000 ÷ 5 years) × 2		

At this point, the book value would be $6,600 ($11,000 cost less $4,400 accumulated depreciation).

In the second year, the depreciation would be $2,640 ($6,600 book value ÷ 5 years × 2). This continues until the book value reaches the residual value, usually in the final year.

Depletion

Depletion is the allocation of the cost of the natural resources (see Example 11.6). Because the resources are extracted at varying amounts, the units-of-production method is used as follows:

Annual depletion = (Cost of the resource – residual value) ×
Units extracted during the year ÷ Estimated units
to be extracted over its useful life

Example 11.6

A gold mine is purchased on April 1 for $500,000. It is expected to have no residual value and contains 2,000 ounces of gold. In the current year, 100 ounces are extracted. The journal entry to record the first-year depletion is as follows:

Date	Account	Debit	Credit
Dec 31	Depletion Expense	25,000	
	Accumulated Depletion		25,000
	Depletion for the year		
	($500,000 × 100 ounces) ÷ 2,000 ounces		

At this point, the book value would be $475,000 ($500,000 cost less $25,000 accumulated depletion).

Disposing of Fixed Assets

Fixed assets can be sold, trashed or abandoned, such as when a computer becomes obsolete (see Example 11.7). When this occurs, the gain or loss on the **disposition** is computed as follows:

Gain (or loss) on disposition = Sale price – Book value

Example 11.7

A piece of equipment is sold on October 1 for $3,000. The equipment cost $11,000 and has an accumulated depreciation of $7,000. The journal entry to record the sale is as follows:

Date	Account	Debit	Credit
Oct 1	Cash	3,000	
	Accumulated Depreciation	7,000	
	Loss on Sale of Equipment	1,000	
	Equipment		11,000
	Show sale of equipment and resulting loss		

The $3,000 sale price less the book value of $4,000 ($11,000 cost – $7,000 accumulated depreciation) results in a loss of $1,000.

Intangible Assets

Intangible assets are items that lack physical substance (i.e., cannot be touched). Examples of some intangible assets, and their lives, are listed here:

- *Patent.* The exclusive right to use, make, sell or control an item or process. Patents are granted for twenty years.
- *Copyright (©).* The right to print, reprint, sell or distribute literary, musical, artistic and similar works. A copyright is valid for the life of the author plus seventy years.
- *Trademark (™).* A name, symbol or other identity given to a company, product or service. While trademarks are only valid for ten years, they can be renewed indefinitely.
- *Customer list.* Names, addresses, contact information and history of business customers. Among other factors, the life of a customer list depends on the length of time of the relationship and the history with the customer.
- *Franchise.* The right to use a name or offer specific services. Franchise agreements are generally for a specific time period. Depending on the franchise, the agreements may continually be renewed.
- *Licenses.* Operating rights granted by a business or governmental entity. Licenses, like franchises, are usually for a specific period but often can be renewed.
- *Goodwill.* The excess of the purchase price over the value of a company that is purchased or otherwise acquired. As long as the acquired business is in operation, goodwill is indefinite.

An intangible asset is amortized using the straight-line method over its estimated useful life (see Example 11.8).

Example 11.8

A company spends $1,000,000 to develop a patent for a new pharmaceutical that is approved on October 1. The patent is expected to last at least 20 years. The journal entry to record the first-year amortization is:

Date	Account	Debit	Credit
Dec 31	Amortization Expense	12,500	
	Patent		12,500
	Amortization for the year		
	($1,000,000 ÷ 20 years) × 3/12		

At this point, the patent will have a value on the books of $987,500 ($1,000,000 cost − $12,500 amortization)

CHAPTER 11 SUMMARY

- Fixed assets generally have long lives and are used in the operations of a company.
- There are three methods to depreciate fixed assets.
- The cost of the use of natural resources is called depletion.
- The book value of an asset is not the same as its actual market value.
- When an asset is sold or otherwise disposed, a gain or loss is recorded.
- Intangible assets are those with no physical substance. The cost is amortized over the useful life of the asset.

CURRENT LIABILITIES AND CONTINGENCIES

This chapter covers liabilities that are due within one year, as well as liabilities that potentially may arise in the future.

Current Liabilities

Current liabilities are obligations that are expected to be paid within one year or the organization's operating cycle, whichever is longer. Conversely, long-term liabilities are those expected to be paid in more than a year.[43] Examples of current liabilities are discussed in this section.

Accounts Payable: Amounts owed from the ongoing operations of an organization (see Example 12.1).

---

[43] Long-term liabilities are discussed in Chapter 13.

Example 12.1

On February 21, an organization places an advertisement for $200, to be paid in 30 days. The entry to record this transaction is as follows:

Date	Account	Debit	Credit
Feb 21	Advertising Expense	200	
	Accounts Payable		200
	Placed an advertisement on account		

When the bill is paid, the entry is as follows:

Date	Account	Debit	Credit
Mar 20	Accounts Payable	200	
	Cash		200
	Paid advertising bill		

Sales Tax: Companies collect sales tax at the time a purchase is made, and, at some later date, send the amount collected to the appropriate governmental entity (see Example 12.2). Sales tax is usually a percent of the sale price and is recorded at the time the sale is made.

Example 12.2

In October, a restaurant has taxable sales of $10,000 and collects sales tax of 8% ($800). The entry to record the monthly sales is as follows:

Date	Account	Debit	Credit
Oct 31	Cash	10,800	
	Sales		10,000
	Sales Tax Payable		800
	Sales and tax collected for the month		

When the taxes are paid to the government the following month, the entry is as follows:

Date	Account	Debit	Credit
Nov 15	Sales Tax Payable	800	
	Cash		800
	Paid sales tax owed		

Customer Deposits: Customers may leave a deposit as a guarantee for performance on a contract, down payment for services, or a guarantee for future payment. Since this deposit may be refunded to the customer, this liability is be recorded (see Example 12.3).

Example 12.3

On October 16, a business receives a $5,000 deposit for containers. The entry to record this transaction is as follows:

Date	Account	Debit	Credit
Oct 16	Cash	5,000	
	Refundable Deposits		5,000
	Receive deposit on containers		

When the containers are returned in December, the entry is as follows:

Date	Account	Debit	Credit
Dec 15	Refundable Deposits	5,000	
	Cash		5,000
	Received containers and refunded customer deposit		

Advance Payments: A customer may make a payment in advance of using a product or service. These are liabilities until the product is delivered or the service is completed (see Example 12.4).

Example 12.4

On December 24, a gift card is purchased for $100. The entry to record this transaction is as follows:

Date	Account	Debit	Credit
Dec 24	Cash	100	
	Deferred Revenue		100
	Gift card sale		

When the card is redeemed in January, the entry is as follows:

Date	Account	Debit	Credit
Jan 2	Deferred Revenue	100	
	Sales		100
	Gift card redeemed		

Payroll-Related Transactions

Bonuses: In addition to either hourly pay or a fixed salary, some companies pay cash bonuses. These can be discretionary or awarded based on performance, customer satisfaction, or other factors. Since a bonus will be paid at a later date, the amount is accrued and shown as a liability (see Example 12.5).

Example 12.5

A sales agent earns a commission for the year of $5,000, to be paid January 31 of the following year. The entry to record this liability is as follows:

Date	Account	Debit	Credit
Dec 31	Salary Expense	5,000	
	Salaries Payable		5,000
	Commission owed to employee		

When the amount is paid in January, the entry is as follows:

Date	Account	Debit	Credit
Jan 15	Salaries Payable	5,000	
	Cash		5,000
	Pay accrued commission		

Payroll Withholdings: Companies are required to withhold a number of items from an employee's pay (see Example 12.6). Legally mandated items include:

- Social Security taxes (FICA);
- Medicare taxes;
- federal income taxes;
- state and local taxes; and
- garnishments.

Other items that may be withheld include:

- health insurance;
- retirement plan contributions; and
- union dues.

For each employee paycheck, the dollar amount of each of these withholdings will vary. In all cases, the amounts must be accumulated and sent to the appropriate authority.

Example 12.6

On April 30, an organization has salaries of $20,000 and withholds $6,000 in payroll taxes, giving the employees checks totaling $14,000. The entry to record the payroll is as follows:

Date	Account	Debit	Credit
Apr 30	Salary Expense	20,000	
	Payroll Taxes Payable		6,000
	Cash		14,000
	Record April 30 payroll		

Employer Taxes: An employer must match the FICA and the Medicare taxes that are withheld from an employee (see Example 12.7). These are added to the withholdings and paid to the government, together with the amounts withheld from the employee's checks, at a later date.

Example 12.7

Using Example 12.6, $1,530 included in the withholdings are FICA and Medicare taxes. The entry to record the employer's share is as follows:

Date	Account	Debit	Credit
Apr 30	Payroll Tax Expense	1,530	
	Payroll Taxes Payable		1,530
	Employer's share of payroll taxes		

When the taxes are paid to the government in May, the entry is as follows:

Date	Account	Debit	Credit
May 15	Payroll Taxes Payable	7,530	
	Cash		7,530
	Taxes paid on April 30 payroll ($6,000 + $1,530)		

Compensated Absences: Companies often grant employees vacation, holidays and sick pay. Of these, only vacation is required to be paid when an employee leaves a job; the rest are generally forfeited. Since this is a future liability, the vacation owed must be accrued (see Example 12.8).

Example 12.8

At the end of the year, an organization has twenty employees who have accumulated a total of $4,000 unused vacation. The journal entry to record this is as follows:

Date	Account	Debit	Credit
Dec 31	Salary Expense	4,000	
	Vacation Payable		4,000
	Vacation owed to employees		

In January, two employees take $300 worth of vacation. The entry is as follows:

Date	Account	Debit	Credit
Jan 31	Vacation Payable	300	
	Cash		300
	Reflect employee vacation		

Contingencies

A loss **contingency** is an existing, uncertain situation involving a potential loss, which depends on whether some future event occurs (see Example 12.9). Some examples are:

- lawsuits;
- IRS audits; and
- environmental issues.

Contingencies are classified and reported in one of three ways:

1. *Probable.* The loss is likely to occur. If the amount can be estimated, an accrual of the potential liability is made; otherwise, only the fact that there is a potential liability is disclosed.
2. *Reasonably possible.* The chance that the loss will occur is possible but not likely. No accrual is made, but the fact is disclosed.
3. *Remote.* The chance of loss is slight. In most cases, no accrual or disclosure is required.

Example 12.9

A company sells a tire with a two-year warranty against defects. Based on past experience, warranty costs are about 2% of annual sales. During the current year, sales were $100,000. The entry to record the contingency is as follows:

Date	Account	Debit	Credit
Dec 31	Warranty Expense	2,000	
	Warranty Liability		2,000
	Record warranty liability ($100,000 × 2%)		

If a customer returns a tire on May 15 for a $100 refund, the entry to record this transaction is as follows:

Date	Account	Debit	Credit
May 15	Warranty Liability	100	
	Cash		100
	Customer refund for returned tire		

At this point, the Warranty Liability account would have a balance of $1,900 ($2,000 – $100 return).

CHAPTER 12 SUMMARY

- Current liabilities are obligations that are expected to be paid within one year or the organization's operating cycle, whichever is longer.
- There are various types of liabilities that must be accrued.
- Employers have payroll withholdings and, together with their share of the taxes, remit these withholdings to the government and other entities.
- Vacation pay owed to employees is accrued.
- Depending on the likelihood of loss, contingent liabilities may have to be accrued and/or disclosed.

LONG-TERM LIABILITIES

T his chapter discusses two types of long-term debt: (1) bonds and (2) notes payable.

Bonds

A **bond** is a form of borrowing used by both businesses and governmental entities. A bond is a formal promise by the issuer to pay the borrowed amount back, plus interest, at some future date. Unlike a note payable, where only one lender is involved, bonds are usually issued in small denominations to many lenders.

There are many different **types** of bonds, some of which are described in the following list:

- *Corporate:* Issued by private and public companies.
- *Governmental:* Issued by governmental entities.
- *Secured:* If the buyer defaults, the bondholders get specific assets of the lender.
- *Unsecured:* The bond is backed only by the creditworthiness of the lender.
- *Term:* The issuer repays the entire amount on a single, specified date.
- *Serial:* The issuer pays back the principal in installments.
- *Callable:* The issuer may, at their option, repay the loan early.
- *Convertible:* The lender has the option to convert the bond to stock.

Sale of Bonds

The issue price of a bond depends on the relation between the market rate and the contract, or stated, rates. The **contract rate** is set when the bond is created, while **the market rate** depends on the bond type and the interest rate at the time the bond is sold.

When the bond is issued, the two rates are frequently different. The contract interest rate is compared with the current market interest rate[44]:

If the contract rate = market rate, the debt is issued at the **face value**.

If the contract rate > market rate, the debt will sell at a **premium**.

If the contract rate < market rate, the debt will sell at a **discount**.

Bonds sold at face value are priced, in bond language, at 100 (i.e., 100%). If a bond is sold at a premium, the proceeds are shown as a number over 100 (e.g., 102, meaning 102% or 1.02) (see Example 13.1). If a bond is sold at a discount, the proceeds are shown as a number under 100 (e.g., 99, meaning 99% or .99).

Example 13.1

On March 31, a company issues a $100,000 5-year corporate bond. The market rate is 4% and the bond pays 3%; the bond is sold at a premium and priced at 102. The entry to record this investment is as follows:

Date	Account	Debit	Credit
Mar 31	Cash	102,000	
	Premium on Bonds Payable		2,000
	Bonds Payable		100,000
	Sale of bond ($100,000 × 1.02)		

Interest

Since bonds are debt, they pay the investor periodic **interest**. The formula to compute interest is as follows:

$$Interest = Face\ value \times contract\ rate \times time\ period$$

If the bond is not issued at face value, the premium or discount is written off (amortized) over the term of the bond (see Example 13.2).

---

[44] Note that these are the exact opposite of how an investor buys bonds, as discussed in Chapter 10.

Example 13.2

Using Example 13.1, when the semi-annual interest is paid on September 30, the entry is as follows:

Date	Account	Debit	Credit
Sep 30	Interest Expense [c]	1,500	
	Premium on Bonds Payable [a]	200	
	Cash [b]		1,700
	Show interest paid on bonds		
	[a] Premium amortization ($2,000 ÷ 10 periods)		
	[b] Six months interest ($100,000 × 3% × 6/12)		
	[c] Interest expense is the sum of these two		

Redemption

If the bond is **redeemed** (such as called) prior to the maturity date, a gain or loss is recognized on the books (see Example 13.3).

Example 13.3

On Sept 30, the company calls the $100,000 bond issued in Example 13.1. Interest rates have dropped, and they call the bond at 99. The entry to record the payment is as follows:

Date	Account	Debit	Credit
Sep 30	Bonds Payable	100,000	
	Premium on Bonds Payable [a]	1,800	
	Cash [b]		99,000
	Gain on Sale of Bond [c]		
	Redemption of bond called at 99		
	[a] Premium balance ($2,000 – $200)		
	[b] Sale price ($100,000 × .99)		
	[c] Difference is the gain on the sale		

Conversion to Stock

If the bond holder exercises their option to convert a bond to capital stock, the capital stock account is credited for the book value at the time of conversion (see Example 13.4). No gain or loss is recognized on the books of the issuer.

Example 13.4

Using Example 13.3, if the bond was converted to stock instead of being redeemed, the entry to record the conversion to stock is as follows:

Date	Account	Debit	Credit
Sep 30	Bonds Payable	100,000	
	Premium on Bonds Payable	1,800	
	Common Stock		101,800
	Show bond converted to common stock		

Installment Notes

Another form of borrowing is a long-term note. This type of financing is typical for real estate, equipment and vehicles. When periodic (usually monthly) payments are made, with each payment generally including both interest and principal, this is called an **installment note** (see Example 13.5).

Example 13.5

On September 30, a company finances a truck for $25,000. The monthly payments, including interest, at 4%, are $471.78 per month for 5 years, at which time the truck is paid off. The entry to record this purchase is as follows:

Date	Account	Debit	Credit
Sep 30	Truck	25,000	
	Note Payable		25,000
	Purchase truck		

Note how just the total amount of the loan is shown. No interest is reflected until a payment is made.

For every payment, both the interest expense and the principal reduction are recorded (see Example 13.6). Thus, over the term of the note, the interest expense will decrease and the amount of principal paid back to the lender will increase.

Example 13.6

Using Example 13.5, the entry to record the first two payments are as follows:

Date	Account	Debit	Credit
Oct 31	Interest Expense [a]	83.33	
	Note Payable [b]	388.45	
	Cash		471.78
	Payment on installment note		
	[a] $25,000 × 4% × 1/12		
	[b] $471.78 – interest of $83.33		

Date	Account	Debit	Credit
Nov 30	Interest Expense [a]	82.08	
	Note Payable [b]	389.70	
	Cash		471.78
	Payment on installment note		
	[a] ($25,000 – $377.08) × 4% × 1/12		
	[b] $471.78 – interest of $82.08		

At this point, the amount owed on the loan is $24,244.58 ($25,000.00 – $377.08 – $378.34). Since the loan will be paid off at the end of the 5-year period, the Note Payable account will end up with a zero balance.

Classification

Long-term notes are shown liabilities on the balance sheet. The amount due within one year or the operating cycle, whichever is longer, is shown as a current liability, while the remainder is shown as a long-term liability.

CHAPTER 13 SUMMARY

- Bonds and installment notes are examples of long-term liabilities.
- Bonds are sold at the market rate, which may differ from the stated (contract) rate.
- Installment notes are loans with payments consisting of both principal and interest.
- Long-term notes are shown on the balance sheet, with the current portion shown separately.

OWNERS' EQUITY AND DISTRIBUTIONS

This chapter discusses accounting for:

- owner's equity in various types of entities;
- transactions involving equity; and
- distributions to owners.

Form of Organization

Owners' equity[45] (also just called equity) is the amount left over when the liabilities are paid from the assets of a business. Or, put simply:

$$Owners' \ equity = Assets - Liabilities$$

The accounting for owners' equity depends on the type of organization. The four major types of organizations are:

- *Proprietorship.* A business that has one owner. The equity section of the proprietorship balance sheet usually has only one account, either called *Owners' Equity* or *Capital*. Frequently, the name of the owner is also shown (e.g., *John Jones, Capital*).

---

[45] Another term for owners' equity is Capital and Stockholders' Equity. The term Net Assets is used on non-profit financial statements.

- *Partnership.* A business with two or more owners. Equity in a partnership also has only one category, generally called *Partners' Capital.* If there are just a few partners, the name of each partner and their capital account balances, rather than the total amount, are shown on the balance sheet.
- *Corporation.* A legal entity separate from its owners. As will be discussed in this chapter, corporations have many parts in the equity section of the balance sheet.
- *LLC or LLP.* An organization that has the characteristics of both a corporation and a partnership. Equity in an LLC usually only has only one category, generally called *Members' Capital.*

Paid-in Capital

An investment in an organization is called **paid-in capital** (see Example 14.1). As illustrated in this section, for all entities except a corporation, the entry credits the owners' equity account.

Example 14.1

On September 1, a proprietorship is formed and the owner invests $1,000 in the business. The entry is as follows:

Date	Account	Debit	Credit
Sep 1	Cash	1,000	
	Owner's Equity		1,000
	Owner's investment in the business		

Because of legal requirements that vary by state, a corporation must separate their paid-in capital into two parts:

1. **Common stock**[46]: The voting shares of a corporation.
2. **Preferred stock**: Stock that has specific rights (preferences) that differ it from common stock. The most common right is priority on the payment of dividends.

---

[46] Sometimes called *Capital Stock.*

Some corporate articles of incorporation assign a **par value** to each share of stock. This is an arbitrary number that has no bearing on the value of the stock but, rather, is a legal requirement of that particular state. Any amount invested above the par value is called **Paid-In Capital in Excess of Par** (see Example 14.2).

Example 14.2

On March 1, a corporation is formed and the owner invests $10,000 in the business by purchasing 100 shares of $1 par value stock. The entry is as follows:

Date	Account	Debit	Credit
Mar 1	Cash	10,000	
	Common Stock [a]		1,000
	Paid-in Capital in Excess of Par [b]		9,000
	Purchase of common stock		
	[a] 100 shares × $1 par value		
	[b] Amount invested less the par value		

Other Comprehensive Income

Other comprehensive income is some revenues, expenses, gains, and losses that are excluded from net income on the income statement. This means that they are instead listed after net income on the income statement.

Examples of items that may be classified as other comprehensive income are:

- unrealized holding gains or holding losses on investments that are classified as available for sale;
- foreign currency translation gains or losses;
- pension plan gains or losses; and
- pension prior service costs or credits.

Treasury Stock

A corporation might buy back its stock and, rather than resell or retire the stock, hold on to the shares. This account, called **Treasury Stock,** is a contra-equity account—that is, an equity account with a debit balance (see Example 14.3).

Example 14.3

On September 1, a corporation repurchases 100 shares of common stock for $5 per share. The entry is as follows:

Date	Account	Debit	Credit
Sep 1	Treasury Stock	500	
	Cash		500
	Repurchase 100 shares at $5 per share		

When a corporation resells their treasury stock, no gain or loss is reflected on the income statement. If the stock is sold at a loss, Retained Earnings is debited. If the stock is sold at a gain, the increase is reflected in the equity section of the balance sheet (see Example 14.4).

Example 14.4

Using Example 14.3, on December 1, 50 shares of the 100 shares of the common stock that were purchased are resold for $6 per share. The entry is as follows:

Date	Account	Debit	Credit
Dec 1	Cash [a]	300	
	Treasury Stock [b]		250
	Paid-in Capital – Treasury Stock [c]		50
	Purchase 50 shares for the treasury		
	[a] 50 shares × $6 per share cost		
	[b] 50 shares × $5 per share cost		
	[c] $300 repurchase price less $250 cost		

At this point, the balance in the Treasury Stock account is $250 ($500 cost less $250 sale).

Distributions

When a company makes a **distribution of profits** to the owners, the accounting for that payment depends on the type of entity. In all cases, these are shown as a reduction in the equity account and never as an expense.

For a proprietorship, partnership and LLC or LLP, these distributions are called **draws** (or drawing). The accounting entry debits the capital account (see Example 14.5).

Example 14.5

On June 1, a proprietorship gives the owner a $750 check for distribution of profits. The entry is as follows:

Date	Account	Debit	Credit
Jun 1	Owner's Equity	750	
	Cash		750
	Cash distribution to the owner		

Cash Dividends

Unlike the other entities, a corporation may only make a distribution to the owners if they have enough accumulated profits, called retained earnings, to make the distribution. These are called **dividends** and can be paid in cash, property or stock (see Example 14.6).

Most dividends are paid in cash. The dividends are recorded as a liability on the date they are approved and announced by the Board of Directors, known as the **declaration date**. At that time, the Board will also announce when the dividends are to be paid, known as the **payment date**.

Example 14.6

On December 10, the Board of Directors declares a $5,000 dividend to be paid on January 15. The entry to record the dividend is as follows:

Date	Account	Debit	Credit
Dec 10	Dividends	5,000	
	Cash Dividends Payable		5,000
	Dividends declared to be paid on January 15		

When the dividend is paid, the entry is as follows:

Date	Account	Debit	Credit
Jan 15 31	Cash Dividends Payable	5,000	
	Cash		5,000
	Payment of dividends declared		

If a company has preferred stock, the holders of the preferred stock get their **preferred dividends** before the common stockholders (see Example 14.7). These can be either cumulative or noncumulative:

- *Cumulative.* If the dividend is not paid, the unpaid amount, called **dividends in arrears**, must be made up in a later year before any other dividends can be paid.
- *Noncumulative.* If the dividend is not paid, no future obligation exists.

Example 14.7

A company has the following capital structure:

Common stock, $1 par value, 500,000 shares outstanding $500,000

5% cumulative preferred stock,

     $10 par value, 10,000 shares outstanding   100,000

In 2020 the Board of Directors declares dividends of $1,000. The preferred stockholders are owed $5,000 (10,000 shares × $10/share × 5%), so they get the entire $1,000. The remaining amount, or $4,000, are in arrears.

In 2021, the Board of Directors declares dividends of $10,000. The preferred stockholders would first receive the $4,000 owed from 2020, plus the $5,000 owed from 2021, for a total of $9,000. The common stockholders would receive the $1,000 remaining amount ($10,000 − $9,000).

Stock Dividends

A Board of Directors may declare a distribution of additional shares to the stockholders. These are called **stock dividends** and are awarded to stockholders in proportion to their holdings (see Example 14.8). For small stock dividends, generally less than 20% of the outstanding shares, the fair value of the stock is used for the accounting entry.

Example 14.8

On May 1, a company awards a 10% common stock dividend on 20,000 shares of $1 par common stock to be distributed on May 15. The market price is $5 per share. The entry to record the dividend is as follows:

Date	Account	Debit	Credit
May 1	Retained Earnings [a]	10,000	
	Stock Dividends Distributable [b]		2,000
	Paid-in Capital in Excess of Par [c]		8,000
	Stock dividends awarded		
	[a] 20,000 shares × 10% dividend × $5 market value		
	[b] 20,000 shares × 10% dividend × $1 par value		
	[c] Difference between the two ($10,000 – $2,000)		

When the stock is distributed, the entry is as follows:

Date	Account	Debit	Credit
May 15	Stock Dividends Distributable	2,000	
	Common Stock		2,000
	Distribution of common stock dividend		

For large stock dividends, generally over 20% of outstanding shares, these are accounted for as stock splits (see the following section).

Stock Splits

A **stock split** is a change in the number of outstanding shares (see Example 14.9). Because the dollar amount of common stock stays the same, no accounting entry is made for stock splits. The only change is the par value of the stock.

Example 14.9

A company has 10,000 shares of $100 par value common stock. Prior to the stock split, the amount of common stock on the balance sheet is $1,000,000 (10,000 shares × $100 par value).

The company declares a 2-for-1 stock split. This means that each shareholder gets an additional share of stock, so instead of the original 10,000 shares outstanding, after the split there will be 20,000 shares outstanding. This changes the par value from $100 per share to $50 per share. The total amount on the balance sheet, $1,000,000 (20,000 shares × new $50 par value) remains unchanged.

CHAPTER 14 SUMMARY

- The form of organization dictates how an organization accounts for the equity section of the balance sheet.
- A corporation may buy back, and resell, Treasury stock.
- Cash distributions are recorded on the declaration date for a corporation and on the payment date for other entities.
- Preferred stockholders get their dividends prior to common stockholders.
- A corporation may also pay stock dividends or declare a stock split.

USING FINANCIAL STATEMENT INFORMATION

This chapter discusses tools that are used to gain a glimpse into the future from past and present data in financial statements.

Financial Statement Analysis

There are generally four ways to analyze financial statements: (1) comparative financial statements; (2) horizontal analysis; (3) vertical analysis; and (4) other.

Comparative financial statements. Certain trends become apparent when comparing financial statements side by side. As shown in the following sample, comparing two periods provides useful insight as to a company's operations.

Sample Corporation
Comparative Income Statements
For the months of July 2019 and 2020

	2019	2020
Sales revenue	$ 45,000	$ 48,500
Cost of goods sold	30,000	32,000
Gross profit	15,000	16,500
Operating Expenses:		
Advertising	200	200
Depreciation	200	200
Insurance	500	700
Rent	1,500	2,000
Payroll taxes	700	800
Salaries	9,000	10,000
Supplies	400	500
Total operating expenses	12,500	14,400
Operating income	2,500	2,100
Provision for income taxes	(400)	(283)
Net income	$ 2,100	$ 1,817

Horizontal analysis. Each item on the financial statement is shown as a percentage of the same item in a *prior period* (known as the **base amount**). As illustrated in the following sample, comparing the balance of sales this year to the same period last year indicates the amount and percent change between the two years.

	2019	2020	$ Change	% Change
Sample Corporation Income Statement: Horizontal Analysis For the month of July 2019 and 2020				
Sales revenue	$ 45,000	$ 48,500	$ 3,500	7.8%
Cost of goods sold	30,000	32,000	2,000	6.7%
Gross profit	15,000	16,500	1,500	10.0%
Operating Expenses:				
Advertising	200	200	-	0.0%
Depreciation	200	200	-	0.0%
Insurance	500	700	200	40.0%
Rent	1,500	2,000	500	33.3%
Payroll taxes	700	800	100	14.3%
Salaries	9,000	10,000	1,000	11.1%
Supplies	400	500	100	25.0%
Total operating expenses	12,500	14,400	1,900	15.2%
Operating income	2,500	2,100	(400)	-16.0%
Provision for income taxes	(400)	(283)	117	-29.3%
Net income	$ 2,100	$ 1,817	$ (283)	-13.5%

Vertical analysis. Each item on the financial statement is shown as a percent of the base amount in the *same period.* As shown in the following sample, showing the cost of goods sold as a percent of sales gives a picture of the profitability of each item sold. Other expenses can also be analyzed in a similar fashion.

	2019		2020	
	Amount	%	Amount	%
Sales revenue	$ 45,000	100.0%	$ 48,500	100.0%
Cost of goods sold	30,000	66.7%	32,000	66.0%
Gross profit	15,000	33.3%	16,500	34.0%
Operating Expenses:				
Advertising	200	0.4%	200	0.4%
Depreciation	200	0.4%	200	0.4%
Insurance	500	1.1%	700	1.4%
Rent	1,500	3.3%	2,000	4.1%
Payroll taxes	700	1.6%	800	1.6%
Salaries	9,000	20.0%	10,000	20.6%
Supplies	400	0.9%	500	1.0%
Total operating expense	12,500	27.8%	14,400	29.7%
Operating income	2,500	5.6%	2,100	4.3%
Provision for income taxes	(400)	-0.9%	(283)	-0.6%
Net income	$ 2,100	4.7%	$ 1,817	3.7%

Title of table:

Sample Corporation
Income Statement: Vertical Analysis
For the month of July 2019 and 2020

Other forms of analysis. Financial statement items are converted to ratios and other formulas to help evaluate the performance and risk of a company. The three categories—liquidity, solvency, and profitability—are described in this chapter.

Liquidity

Liquidity is the ability of a company to convert its assets to cash and pay its current bills. This gives a general idea of the organization's ability to meet its short-term obligations as they come due. Some of the most common ratios are listed here.

Current Ratio: Probably the most commonly used ratio, the **current ratio** is the ratio of current assets to current liabilities. This gives an indication as to whether a company can pay its bills in the coming year. The higher the current ratio, the more likely the organization is to be able to pay its bills. The formula is as follows:

$$Current\ Ratio = Current\ assets \div Current\ Liabilities$$

Quick Ratio: Current assets include some items that will not be converted to cash, such as prepaid expenses and inventory. The **quick ratio** (also called the **acid test**) evaluates assets that are readily available to pay current liabilities. As with the current ratio, the higher the ratio, the more likely the organization will be to pay its bills. The formula is as follows:

$$Quick\ Ratio = Cash + Short\text{-}term\ Investments +$$
$$Accounts\ Receivable \div Current\ Liabilities$$

Current Debt Coverage: An organization's liquidity depends on whether it can generate enough cash to make its debt payments to lenders. The **current debt coverage ratio** measures whether or not a company generates enough cash from operating activities to pay its debt; the higher the ratio, the more likely they will be able to meet future debt payments. The formula is as follows:

$$Current\ Debt\ Coverage = Cash\ Provided\ by\ Operating\ Activities \div Average\ Current\ Liabilities^{47}$$

Solvency

Solvency is the ability of a company to pay its long-term bills. These analytics measure an organization's likelihood of being able to meet its future obligations.

Debt to Equity Ratio: The **debt-to-equity ratio** shows the proportion of liabilities to the company's equity, showing how much an organization relies on debt financing. The higher the ratio, the riskier their solvency. The formula is as follows:

$$Debt\ to\ Equity = Total\ Liabilities \div Total\ Stockholders'\ Equity$$

---

[47] Average is computed by adding the beginning balance plus the ending balance and dividing by 2.

Times Interest Earned: **Times interest earned** measures the company's profit before income taxes to see what is available to make required interest payments. The higher the ratio, the more likely that the company will be able to pay the interest on time. The formula is as follows:

Times Interest Earned = Net Income before Interest and Taxes ÷ Interest Expense

Cash Debt Coverage: This ratio measures the company's ability to pay its debts with cash provided from operating activities. The higher the **cash debt coverage**, the better off the company is to pay its obligations. The formula is as follows:

Cash Debt Coverage = Cash Provided by Operating Activities ÷ Average Total Liabilities

Free Cash Flow: **Free cash flow** is not a ratio but, rather, a measure of the cash that a company has which they can use to invest in fixed assets, pay off debt or pay dividends. The formula is as follows:

Free Cash Flow = (Cash Provided by Operating Activities –
Capital Expenditures – Cash Dividends)

Profitability

Profitability measures the company's ability to earn an adequate return on its sales and assets. These analytics measure how well a business is meeting those objectives.

Profit Margin: The **profit margin** shows the portion of each dollar of revenue, after expenses have been paid, that is available for other purposes, such as purchasing fixed assets, paying off debt or declaring dividends.[48] The higher the profit margin, the more funds are generated. The formula is as follows:

Profit Margin = Net Income ÷ Net Sales

---

[48] Part of this computation is the same as vertical analysis, discussed earlier.

Asset Turnover: The **asset turnover ratio** measures a company's efficiency in using assets to generate revenue. This is a broad measure of how efficient a company is in using their assets. The formula is as follows:

$$Asset\ Turnover\ Ratio = Net\ Sales \div Average\ Total\ Assets$$

Accounts Receivable Turnover: The **accounts receivable turnover ratio** is an indication of how quickly, and efficiently, a company is able to collect money from its customers. The higher the ratio, the shorter the average time period between the sale and the cash collection. The formula is as follows:

$$Accounts\ Receivable\ Turnover\ Ratio = Net\ Credit\ Sales \div$$
$$Average\ Accounts\ Receivable$$

In addition to this, many companies look at the **average collection period** of their accounts receivable. This indicates how many days, on average, amounts are owed to the company. The formula is as follows:

$$Average\ Collection\ Period = 365\ days \div$$
$$Accounts\ Receivable\ Turnover\ Ratio$$

Inventory Turnover: The **inventory turnover ratio** shows how quickly inventory is sold. The more frequently a business can sell (turn over) its inventory, the more cash it has for other purposes. The higher the ratio, the more efficient a company is. The formula is as follows:

$$Inventory\ Turnover\ Ratio = Cost\ of\ Goods\ Sold \div$$
$$Average\ Inventory\ Balance$$

Similar to accounts receivable, many companies look at **average days in inventory**. This shows the average number of days it normally takes to sell inventory. The formula is as follows:

$$Average\ Days\ in\ Inventory = 365 \div Inventory\ Turnover\ Ratio$$

Return on Assets: The **return on assets** (also called ROA) indicates the earning power of the company's assets. Since this varies among various lines of business, a company will generally compare their return on assets with the industry averages to help evaluate their performance. The formula is as follows:

$$Return\ on\ Assets = Net\ Income \div Average\ Total\ Assets$$

Return on Equity: Since stockholders are interested in how management uses their money to generate a profit, the **return on equity** (also called ROE) is computed. The formula is as follows:

$$Return\ on\ Equity = Net\ Income \div Average\ Total\ Equity$$

CHAPTER 15 SUMMARY

* There are four techniques an organization can use to analyze how they are doing.
* Liquidity analysis looks at the ability of a company to convert its assets to cash and pay its current bills.
* Solvency analysis looks to see if the company can pay its long-term obligations.
* Profitability analysis looks at the company's ability to earn an adequate return on its sales and assets.

INDEX

ABOUT THE AUTHOR

In 1979, Howard J. Levine formed an accounting firm in the Los Angeles area. Until its sale in 2016, the office was well known for bookkeeping, accounting, tax return preparation, tax planning and consulting for small businesses, partnerships and corporations, as well as tax-exempt (nonprofit) organizations and private foundations.

As a college professor and in private practice, plus with experience with national accounting firms, Howard created a diverse client base and a wealth of experience, providing accounting and tax services to a unique group of clients nationwide. These clients ranged from small retail businesses, physicians, restaurants and a variety of service businesses, to nonprofit organizations and private foundations with budgets from under $100,000 to assets over $100 million.

Howard has served as both a member and Southern California coordinator of the Technical Review Panel of the California Board of Accountancy. He has written questions used on the CPA examination and has served on the board of numerous organizations as board member, treasurer and president. Howard served as a trustee of the California Society of CPAs Group Insurance Trust and as a member of the Internal Revenue Service Taxpayer Advocacy Panel.

Howard is currently a professor of accounting at Los Angeles Valley College. He is a CPA as well as a diplomat and life member of the American Board of Forensic Accountants.

OTHER BOOKS BY HOWARD J. LEVINE:

Accounting Ethics: A Practical Approach

It's Your Money: What Everybody Needs to Know about Personal Finance

The Greatest Book Ever Written: What the Bible Is Telling Us Today

www.ingramcontent.com/pod-product-compliance
Lightning Source LLC
Chambersburg PA
CBHW080624030426

42336CB00018B/3074